Shanta Rameshwar Rao was born in Mercara and educated in Patna, Lucknow and Hyderabad. She lives and works in Hyderabad where she founded and now directs the Vidyaranya School.

Mrs. Rameshwar Rao writes mainly for children. Her *Tales of Ancient India* has been reprinted several times and has also been published in the UK. Her version of *The Mahabharata* was originally published in an edition for children and an adapted edition of this, as also her stories on the myths of legends of India, were reissued with illustrations by the famous painter Badri Narayan. *Children of God,* her first novel, was published by Sangam Books in 1976 and was instantly acclaimed as 'a remarkable attempt for a first novel.'

Children of God

Shanta Rameshwar Rao

Disha Books

Disha Books
an imprint of

ORIENT LONGMAN LIMITED

Registered office
3-6-272 Himayatnagar, Hyderabad 500 029

Other Offices
Kamani Marg, Ballard Estate, Bombay 400 038
17 Chittaranjan Avenue, Calcutta 700 072
160 Anna Salai, Madras 600 002
1/24 Asaf Ali Road, New Delhi 110 002
80/1 Mahatma Gandhi Road, Bangalore 560 001
3-6-272 Himayatnagar, Hyderabad 500 029
Birla Mandir Road, Patna 800 004
S.C. Goswami Road, Panbazar, Guwahati 781 001
'Patiala House', 16-A Ashok Marg, Lucknow 226 001

© Orient Longman Limited 1976
Reprinted 1992
ISBN 0 86311 190 4

Phototypeset by
Pratikshan Publications Pvt. Ltd
7 J. N. Road
Calcutta 700 013

Printed in India at
Swapna Printing Works (P) Ltd.
52 Raja Rammohan Roy Sarani
Calcutta 700 009

Published by
Orient Longman Limited
17 Chittaranjan Avenue
Calcutta 700 072

To
Rameshwar
with love

Introduction

I had started writing the *Children of God* in 1954, but like most novels it had been growing inside me decades before that year. When I finally put pen to paper in 1954 and started to write I was suddenly staggered and bewildered by the enormity of the task I had undertaken. I realized painfully that whatever I wrote, however feelingly I wrote, it was pale and lifeless beside the living images inside me of the character 'Lakshmi' and her family of untouchable scavenger people. For they were a close and intrinsic part of me and my childhood and growing-up years. As a child I had never been able to get away from them : whenever I could I would engage in conversation with them from my side of the invisible and powerful barrier that separated us. And sometimes I stood outside their homes in the untouchable quarter watching the goings on in the everyday life so different from mine.

As I worked at the book (writing one day, tearing up the next, vowing never to write and yet compelled by a fierce inner need to start all over again), I realized that it was really my story and the story of my growing up that I was struggling to tell. In some inner region of childhood their story and mine had become one, as I listened to the stories the many 'Lakshmis' used to tell, as I stood for hours on the steps of the temple, watching the 'Siddas' and their families collect the leavings, and as I stood some way away from the shrines of the spirits watching the ritual dances and sacrifices. The temple which they may not enter was part too of my every day life as were the stories that were told by my many, many friends of the saints who saw the truth and the false and lived without the illusory barriers that thought had erected over centuries. Wherever I went and whatever I did the faces of 'Lakshmi' and her family haunted me and would not let me be. In the book they are imaginary characters, but they are grounded firmly in the reality I perceived in the clear vision of a child.

But even as I was writing and telling our story—Lakshmi's and mine—the world had changed. It was continually changing. But in spite of all the changes the central issue remained unchanged. It is true that over the years we have learnt, at least in theory that no human being may be regarded as untouchable. It is true too that our constitution decrees that it is a crime to deny a fellow human being the right to be fully human. These are important achievements. But the canker of the issue remains unsolved. It has assumed new dimensions and contours. Today we have witnessed untold horrors since the time 'Kittu' was done to death and 'Lakshmi and Mada' wept for him. Violence continues and is with us wherever we go. Time has made little difference.

'Lakshmi's grandchildren and mine will no doubt tell their own stories which will be different from this one which I have told and which is hers and mine—ours. But the threads that tie those stories to this are not broken so easily. Their story or stories are a continuation—and their end is still nowhere in sight.

Shanta Rameshwar Rao.

The women are around me, weeping aloud, crying out the name of Kittu again and again. Soma is weeping too. I have never seen Soma weeping before. But today her tears are flowing. Mada, my husband and Kittu's father is sitting beside me. His body shakes with sobs, and his face is contorted with misery.

They have laid out Kittu's charred remains on the earth. My hands are cold; inside me all is darkness. The weeping women, the blackened mass of flesh before me—all are like figures in a dream. How can it be that this fearful thing from which the burnt skin hangs out like loose clothing, was, a few hours ago, Kittu—a man who lived and breathed and walked and talked—a fully grown man, twenty-five years old—as old as the Independence of our country?

The year that Kittu was born was the year of our freedom. There was great rejoicing at the time of his birth. And when he was fully a year old he went with us, straddling my hip, to Venugopalapuram to watch the festivities. There were flags flying and music playing. Someone had bought all the balloons from a balloon seller and distributed them among the children in the street. There were crowds of people pushing and jostling towards the *maidan*. Garlanded leaders were making loud speeches with much gesticulation. Kittu watched all with big eyes. He was a happy child, never fretful or peevish. He laughed to see the flags and balloons and clapped his hands when he heard the music. When my arms grew tired, Mada took him from me. After a while Kittu fell asleep on his father's shoulder.

It is many years since freedom and Kittu's birth; many years since our flag was raised and honoured and many longer years since Gandhi the Mahatma fasted that the temple doors may be opened to the untouchable people. But Kittu, the untouchable boy, my only son was done to death because he dared to enter the Temple.

"All men will be equal in free India," they told us, at the time when we gained our Independence: "the divisions of caste will be closed and no man will be untouchable." But you cannot change the hearts of men.

"Now we are free." The politicians shouted, "And the law will protect all, even the poorest and the meanest, against wrong-doing. It will be a crime from now on to call a man an untouchable or to treat him as such. That is the meaning of freedom—that all men will be as brothers and all will be equal."

They spoke very loudly. "Kittu will go to school," I said to Mada. "He will never, never be untouchable any more." "That will be a good thing," said Mada. "Perhaps he will grow learned and wise. Perhaps his learning will bring him wealth." And now Kittu is dead, because he entered the Temple which many years ago had been declared open to all people. His remains lie before me and I can smell the burnt flesh. He grew neither rich nor learned. And the howling mob that beat and stoned and burnt him to death danced around him, while the flames consumed him, and cried out. "Untouchable, untouchable, cleaner of filth, do you dare to defile men of caste?"

They beat him and stoned him and sent him to his death. Some of the men belonged, they say, to the new political party. The new party had been formed to protect the rights of the orthodox, to keep religion pure and to bring back righteousness into the world. Not many people belonged to the party, but many discussed with sympathy the dangers of allowing the lower castes and the untouchables to be infected with the ideas that Gandhi had propagated. "Today they will ask to sit alongside of us and enter our temples; tomorrow they will want to supplant us, take our land and marry our daughters—what then?" they said.

"What then?" they echoed and re-echoed.

And they frowned on the changes that were coming into the life of Venugopalapuram. They frowned on untouchables who went into places where they were forbidden.

And as long as the untouchable folk bowed down without murmur all went well. But Kittu went into the Temple to see the idol of which he had heard and to worship before it, because he was young and unthinking. And his entry was noticed and he was warned. Kittu said: "But the Temple is God's house. And there is a law against untouchability—"

"You are over-stepping the bounds," said the men who belonged to the new party, "You had better have a care." Kittu did not have a care. He was very young and very unthinking. He wore white clothes which were washed and he wore sandals on his feet, forgetting his untouchable state, forgetting that an untouchable may not wear clothes washed too white and sandals on his feet. He would not be warned. And as he came out from the Temple that day a woman saw him and questioned him.

"The Temple is open to all," Kittu answered her. "I went in to make an offering of bananas and—"

The woman grew hysterical with anger at this because when he spoke he looked her in the face, not remembering his untouchable state.

"How can I bear this dishonour?" she shrieked. "The untouchable, the scavenger looks me in the face and talks directly to me. Oh how can I live after this?"

"Beat him," said a boy from the crowd and the crowd howled: "Yes, yes, beat him until he learns his lesson."

"These people understand only one language," someone cried, and the crowd advanced upon him. In their hands were sticks and rods and bars. With loud whoops and screeches they began to belabour him. He cried out for mercy. They had no mercy. They tied him up to the great peepul tree in the temple yard. He howled and bellowed like a wild animal. "You, untouchable, you," they cried: "you bastard, you grow big with the rice you eat: you swell with pride until the earth cannot bear your weight. You will pay the price of your insolence."

And all the while they continued to beat him. Then three men staggered forward arm in arm, and stood before him in menacing postures.

"I have an idea," one said. He made his way through the crowd and disappeared. When he returned some time later, he was carrying a tin of kerosene oil with him.

"See," he laughed "for untouchables who rise above themselves there is only thing to do," while the crowd continued to beat Kittu and the women screamed and danced around him.

"Come," cried the drunk, "just watch me. I know how to deal with these outcastes."

With a terrible cry, he emptied the oil on Kittu.

"Now—now—now," sang the others in unison. "Now the pariah will know." And they set Kittu's clothes on fire. Kittu's screams tore the air. "Never—never more—" he screamed. But the flames rose while he screamed and struggled and the crowd swirled round him in a frenzied, savage dance.

A crowd of people had done this. Their faces, grinning and their teeth bared, their dancing, stamping feet all looked alike. Then a man came running that way. He heard the screaming and the shouting and went to the spot and saw what had happened. The man who was not part of the frenzied crowd called out for order and silence. Suddenly the swirling madness came to an end: the people who had done it stood still and faced their deed. Kittu was screaming still, but his voice had grown hoarse now. He had crumpled up against the tree.

"He must be taken to the hospital," said the man, "but before that there must be a policeman or there will be trouble."

The crowd stared at him. They were frightened now. Their faces were sullen. The woman said defiantly: "He was an untouchable and he defiled the temple." Meanwhile people came running to our quarters calling to me to come.

"It is Kittu—Kittu," they shrieked, and my blood froze. They would not speak coherently. I clutched at a wall for support. "Is he—is he dead?" I asked at last, and to this all-important question they made no answer. So I repeated my question again and again until Soma answered at last in a voice that we could scarcely hear:

"See, there he is. They are lifting him out from the rickshaw there."

Terror whirled in my head, and for a second all grew black before my eyes. Then through a haze I saw them lift the body and bring it towards me. Hands pressed my shoulders down and forced me to sit. Someone was sitting beside me and great sobs were racking him. It was Mada. My eyes saw that it was Mada but he seemed not to belong to me anymore. He, like all things there, seemed not to have any meaning. The sound of wailing and weeping came from far, far, far away. I stare and stare and I have no tears, no grief, no anger, no fear or passion. There is a heaviness in my heart that I must carry inside me all my life.

People crowd around me. There are many familiar faces, but many more are the faces of strangers who have hurried to us on hearing the news of Kittu's death. The story of his burning outside the Temple has spread everywhere. It is a political event. At the funeral there are newspaper men who ply me with endless questions. Was he my only son? How old was he? What did he say before he went? What is my opinion about untouchability? Is it true that I worked for temple entry with the Gandhian Satyagrahis? What methods do I suggest for the eradication of untouchability?

On and on endlessly, and I have no answers, but I must answer nevertheless for they are persistent. Suddenly we have been raised to a position of importance, Mada and I and our dead son, Kittu. There are long speeches made over the scorched body that was Kittu's, about brotherhood and the dignity of man and about the Constitution. There are speeches made for and speeches made against the Government. "There is no hope," the leader of one group shouts, "there is no hope until this Government is removed and our own party is raised to office."

In my ears the words sound hollow and insubstantial: what has Government to do with it all? Kittu, my son, my child is dead. He died a cruel, horrible death. He was bound to a tree and beaten. His clothes were set ablaze. The flames consumed him while he still lived and breathed. The thought of his torment sears my heart. What, oh what, has Government to do with it? If men's hearts are cruel then what does it matter what Government rules? And if another Government should come to rule, will it, can it, restore to me my son? Or wipe out the past?

The men lift the flower-bedecked bier. I rise to my feet. Mada walks before the bier. I walk with the wailing women, and, as I walk, the past and the present detach themselves from me, and move before my eyes. Time loses meaning: memory-ghosts of people come before me; I hear their voices. The days of my childhood in this same untouchable quarter of Venugopalapuram, where our people lived, rise before me.

Always, as far back as they could remember, our people, the scavengers have lived here, far from the dwellings of the caste people. It is a temple town, our Venugopalapuram, and it stands on the river Vasumati. Today a great dam strides the river and the land beneath the dam is rich and fertile. But in the days when I was young this dam had not been built, and there was no lake. There were smaller ones built by the old kings of Venugopalapuram. In the summer the river flowed in a thin little muddy trickle. The rocks grew so hot it seemed that they would blister and burst. But when the rains came, the Vasumati waters grew dark and foamed. They rose and overflowed her banks and caused floods. When she rose in a flood, in her anger the river always brought cholera, the purging and vomiting sickness.

On the other side of the river is Manur with its temple of the Goddess Narayani. Each year the Deity of the Venugopalapuram temple is taken in festive procession over the bridge and the marriage is celebrated between him and the Manur goddess. Trade between Manur and Venugopalapuram is brisk and continuous, and over the bridge go buses and lorries and creaking bullock carts laden with merchandise. In Manur too are the hospital and school of the Mission people.

The temple is the centre of our town and the untouchables' quarter is about a mile away from the temple. Every day we set out with broom and pan from here to clean the latrines of Venugopalapuram. Our people have done this for generations because this is our caste: we are scavengers.

Our fathers and grandfathers and all our forefathers who went before us, have been scavengers and therefore untouchable, and of all the untouchables, we who clean the latrines and carry human filth, we are among the lowliest. No one will associate with us—neither the tanners nor the toddy tappers, nor the glass-cutters, who, though they all belong to the untouchable caste themselves, are still considered to be above us. But we, the scavengers of human filth, are far down on the ladder of untouchability and our homes are farthest from the town and where the caste people live. They are mud huts with roofs of thatch. But thatch costs money and so when it wears away, the roofs are patched with sacking or palm or cardboard or tin—anything that is, for the moment, at hand and available. The floors are mud, and on the walls are pictures of gods and goddesses in different postures, torn from books found in dust heaps. They smile benignly upon the humans in the hole or lift up their hands to bless. They smile endlessly with their red bow-shaped lips and they speak not a word. We join our hands to them and cry out our prayers to them, but the gods do not move or stir.

The doors of our homes are low openings and outside is the narrow untouchables' lane, dusty and dry in the summer and pitted with stagnant pools of water during the rains. Here, the naked children roll over each other and play their games during the daytime. There is a mango tree beneath which the elders of our community meet to talk of important matters concerning the community, and a few paces away from the tree is the water hole from which our people draw water. In the days when I was a child no one came to our quarters except the men sent to vaccinate us against sicknesses—especially small-pox, the fever of the great Mother. But time has brought changes, and today there are people who come to our quarters to talk to us—"Untouchables may claim their rights," they tell us. "Give us your votes and we will bring you your rights!"

Just as people from outside have come in, so too there have been young folk among us, who have wandered away from our midst, in the effort to step out of the pattern of our untouchable existence. There is a discontent gnawing at the core of their beings, and a restlessness in their souls which will not let them be. They leave the homesteads of their fathers and go searching. Such were Boda and Sidda, my brothers. And such too was Kittu my son, though he did not go far. In my time I too struggled in my own way to free myself from the pattern of my untouchable existence. But it seems that an eternity has flowed between the shores of that time and this. I was young then and full of dreams of breaking the prison bars, and emerging into the morning sunlight of freedom. I was full of dreams as I trotted along beside my mother when she went to work. My earliest memories are of walking alongside her. As I grew a little older I learned to keep an eye on the younger ones and carried the youngest on my hip. I can remember how we children stood on the edge of the street in a little cluster and waited while my mother collected human filth from the latrines in her zinc bucket.

I can remember my mother now, a lean, gaunt woman with hollowed cheeks and tangled hair and tired eyes that contained in their depths a vast and endless patience. Never have I seen a woman as patient as my mother was. In her eyes was the thousand year-old patience of our people. There was never any anger in those eyes, no mockery, no bitterness: only patience—the vast unending patience that came from generations and generations of mute, unquestioning suffering. She spoke little and when she spoke, it was most often to beg pardon for her sins, even for her very existence; to call the blessings of heaven upon those who abused her and called her unclean and untouchable.

My father beat her every day. He came in reeking of drink, and lifted up his clenched fists and beat her, and holding her hair in his hand, dashed her head against the wall, demanding money from her to buy him his toddy. She bore everything in silence, believing it to be part of the burden of life.

Unfailingly, each year, my mother grew big with child, and walked with pain and weariness; I helped her then to scavenge and to lift the buckets and take them away. When the pains set in with the cramps and the cold sweat, then I knew, and I ran to get old Granny Ponchu to help her. If it happened at night I woke up the others and hurried them out of the hut. Only once did I allow them to stay when the baby was born; that was a night of driving rain and we could not go out. Frightened and trembling, we saw the birth of a new life before our eyes. But at other times we went out of the door of the hut, listening to the sound of our mother's moaning. And I, sick with dread and anxiety, prayed softly to Mariamma to spare my mother and not let her die. My brothers and sisters stayed near me, whimpering and uneasy,—all but my brother Boda. Boda stood away and would not betray his feelings. He would avert his eyes from mine, and bite his lip and trace circles in the dust with his toe. After long waiting we would hear with relief the first cry: a welcome cry it was to us, and when it came, for some reason we were sure that our mother would not die. That cry was to us the signal that our lives could start to move in their accustomed paths, that all was well again.

Ponchu would bring the newborn out, and display it before us. "Another one!" she would cackle, pride shining in her face, "A boy this time (or girl) and an ugly child it is—small and dark and hairy like a baby monkey." She did not believe what she said of course, nor did we, but there was the evil eye to ward off. One could not be too careful.

I lifted up the second youngest in my arms, for when my mother gave birth to a child, then the second youngest became my charge and from then on, it was I who must care for him. I must take him with me on my hip, carry him wherever I went. He would lose now his sole right to our mother's breasts. He must share them with the newcomer. Soon, very soon, he must yield them completely to the little one. We crowded round Ponchu to see the baby—all except Sidda, my second brother, who would slink away muttering. But Boda came, his anger and hostility gone for a few moments while he looked shyly into the small, wrinkled face. Sometimes he put out his hand and touched the child's cheek softly with his forefinger: there was a look of wonder in his eyes, of love and infinite tenderness. He was a strange boy, my brother Boda, and strange too were the ways in which his destiny took him.

Sidda stayed silent as long as Ponchu was there, but when we were by ourselves Sidda would mutter—not to me, but within my hearing—"What is it but one more mouth to feed—one more belly crying with hunger?" Then he slunk away and hid himself.

My mother had given birth thirteen times, but there were only six of us who lived. Four of my mother's children had died at birth, and one had wasted away until there was nothing left of his blood but water, and then his life had gone. And two had been stricken with the cholera. In the morning when my mother had gone to work they had been well. But when she returned they were stricken with the disease and their purging seemed to bring out their entrails.

They were rolling about on the floor with cramps in their bellies and sweat streaming down their bodies. "Go," my mother whispered to me, "first go and call Ponchu, tell her she must come. And after that, run, child, run to Mariamma and pray. Pray for their lives; pray with all your strength. Offer the Goddess oil and flowers. Promise her a cock—a sheep, a goat, if the children should be spared. Pray, pray, child, pray with all your might for Mariamma's mercy."

Ponchu came with her spells and incantations, her jingling bells of brass, her shells, her seed pods and her icons. For Ponchu knew magic and practised it. But the cramps grew worse and presently their bodies began to convulse and twitch; the limbs began to get cold and the mouths grew dry and the tongues hung out and the drops of water that we gave them trickled from the corner of the grey lips. Through the night we watched to ward off the spirits of death, and in the morning I ran again to Mariamma's shrine to implore her mercy. But the Goddess was deaf. She was made of stone smeared over with orange paint, and her ears were of stone. She would not heed my prayer, and when I came back I found that my brother's life had gone. And the other, the girl, was in the grip of her final agony.

The men brought the bamboos and string to make the bier. The women came with flowers and red powder, and adorned it. Someone said: "Is it not two biers that must be made?" At that my mother cried out: "Oh, Mariamma, the little girl is alive yet—she is alive and may yet recover!" But she did not recover: my mother's hopes were shortlived, and the second bier was put together before the first had reached the burial place. The spirits were hungry that day. My mother shed silent tears and then she made her way to the shrine of Mariamma to pray.

Children of God

The next year there came the visitation of the Goddess of small-pox: and Puttu and Gopu were struck down. They rolled about on the floor of the hut, their bodies covered with running sores that looked like evil flowers of death. They rolled about in agony on the mud floor of the hut and my mother sacrificed a cock this time to Mariamma; but death had laid his invisible finger upon our homestead again. Gopu died, and from Puttu the Goddess snatched an eye. And the marks of her fingers remained on his face for life. After this the men from the municipality came and demanded that all the people in the locality be given the Goddess through vaccination. They seized us and pricked our arms and the Goddess entered our bodies. After that there were no more epidemics.

In Mariamma my mother found comfort and peace. Daily at twilight she would visit the shrine of the Goddess-mother whom our people worshipped. We children went with her and stood clustered round while she called out to the Goddess to protect us with her grace. In the flickering light of the wick lamps the unsculpted stone seemed to move and to smile at us in response to our mother's call. We joined our hands and prayed with all the strength and innocence of our hearts. The lights threw shadows on the walls and our hearts were full of awe. "Mariamma, Goddess all powerful, eternal, terrible, beautiful—O Mariamma, have mercy!" We knew that hers was the spawning womb out of which all things from the greatest to the least, had issued. We knew that she was the fearful Goddess before whom heaven and earth shook; that she had existed before time had begun, before the universe had been fashioned by the hands of the Creator.

When Mariamma was at peace, and her belly was full, then we knew there was nothing as beautiful as she: no mother was kinder, none gentler; all peace emanated from her, all gifts came from her. But when she was angry, when her belly was unsatisfied, then she could, with less than the movement of an eyelid shatter to fragments the earth and all things in it. Yes, and all the worlds beyond it. If she was at peace then Mariamma's arms protected. But if she was angered or wounded, then she could reduce the mountains to sand and the moon and stars to dust; she could uproot the trees of the forests and dry up the waters of the earth at their source. There were times, they said, when in her anger she broke out of her stone prison and went wandering over the countryside. She caused the storms and the winds to blow. She made the river waters rise. She trampled fields and forests underfoot, and released the demons of famine and illness among the people to collect her tribute in human lives.

The lives that were lost, they said, were the lives of those whom she had marked with her finger. At such times there were many who claimed that they had seen her, wandering over the countryside, emerging from within the rocks and trees, and walking on the waters of the river. They swore they had seen her yellow robes and dark hair flying in the wind, her red tongue hanging out of her hungry mouth, the flash of her white teeth.

My mother prayed to Mariamma, knowing that in the end only she was real and all other things illusion. Unfailingly she brought to the shrine offerings bought from her earnings, oil for Mariamma's lamp, flowers, a banana or two, sugar and incense sticks. Her faith in Mariamma's power and goodness was unshakeable. "Mariamma, protect us...forgive our sins," my mother whispered a hundred times a day. "Mariamma, have mercy on us. Give us rice! O Mariamma! Beautiful Mother!" We children clasped our hands and echoed her words. She bought us charms and talismans and scapulars and sacred ash from Mariamma's priests and wandering holy men. "Mariamma will protect you and keep you from harm," she said as she strung them round our necks, wrists and waists, and we felt the protecting hand of the Goddess about us.

The past rises up before me as Kittu's body is lowered into its grave, and as the people dance the funeral dance. The drums are pounding and the dance will continue till late into the night. There will be drinking and singing for the peace of Kittu's spirit. From where I sit I can see the men's feet thumping on the floor. It is like a festival. I see my father among the dancers. He is old now and white-haired, but a dance is a dance and he will not stay away. Besides, this is his own grandson. Whenever there was a festival or a birth, it was my father who always led the dancing. The biggest and most important occasion was the festival of the Goddess Mariamma. It came round three times a year and the untouchable folk from many miles around gathered at the Venugopalapuram shrine for the celebration. We went too. My mother would gather us all together and we would troop to the shrine. There was a fair outside the shrine and my brothers and sisters spoke of nothing but of the fair and the sugary sweets that were sold in the stalls. Soma bought bright pink ribbons and celluloid clips for her hair. But my mind from the first was intent upon the dancing at the shrine. There would be the Great Dance of Mariamma, and my father was always the principal dancer. There was no one, people said, who could dance as well as he and from the surrounding villages they came flocking in their hundreds to see him dance the dance of Mariamma and to hear the voice of the Goddess from his throat. For, when the dance was at its height, the Goddess entered his body and possessed him and spoke through his lips.

I remember now those evenings and the daylight softly flushing with the sunset. I remember how as the twilight deepened I felt the excitement mount inside me. There was a spell on everything, as if by some god's touch all had changed and acquired a new quality—or perhaps it was the sound of the drums. Across the dying day, and the unborn night they would sound, softly at first, and a quiver would go through my body. Then, as if at the voice of the drums, the stars would appear one by one. As the drums grew louder the people heard them and their blood grew restless in their bodies. Then the darkness sprang out like black panthers from behind the hills and the drums quickened. Their wild rhythm gathered intensity and power; they set the night quivering. People began to pour out of their huts, and hurried breathlessly along, carried forward towards the shrine as if on a rushing tide.

My father did not begin his dance till the moon had risen over the hills, and we waited with the crowd, eager and expectant. I could hear the jangling of his waist bells; I could discern movements in the shadows. The smoke from the torches curled upward while minor dancers contorted around us. All the while the drums continued, soft one moment, roaring out the next, until the hills echoed with their rhythm. The priests brought the Goddess round in circumambulation—not the great Goddess of rock who stood in the shrine but another one, a smaller stone, but charged, they said, with the same power as the first. They put her down beneath the tree, and at that moment the moon rose and my father leaped out of the shadows with a piercing yell—"O Mariamma! O Mariamma!" and began to dance. His steps were slow and measured at first. With eyes closed, and lips parted, he was like a sleepwalker. The drums responded to his mood. They grew soft and slow. They murmured to him, gently at first with a loving tenderness. Then, gathering strength, they began to mock and taunt him. They dared him and challenged him. The drum beats entered his body, seeped into his blood, became one with him. His eyes opened; they glittered like jewels. The tip of his tongue showed through his halfopen mouth. In and out of light and shadow he wove his magic dance, calling out again and again in his terrible tortured voice to the Goddess to enter his body. He changed as he danced: from man he changed to panther, and crouched ready to spring upon his prey. From panther he became a stag, from stag he changed to bull, and from bull to deadly hooded snake. The pipes began to play and suddenly he was set spinning and spinning in wild abandon, and in that final dance all things merged to become one, and the anguished voice broke out of his throat again: "O Mariamma, Mariamma," and the Goddess entered his body. We knew the moment: the bonds that connected him with the things of the earth snapped at this point. He ceased to be father and husband. He ceased to be scavenger and untouchable. Power filled him, and when they brought live coals and spread them in his path, he walked upon them and felt nothing.

And now people began to move forward and to whisper to the priests the questions that troubled them. Even people of caste came with their questions. The priest in turn put the questions to the Goddess who possessed my father's body. Her voice spoke through him and answered them and foretold the future. It was now that the priest of Mariamma lifted up his voice and prayed to her and craved her mercy.

"O Mariamma, O Mariamma! yellow-robed and bejewelled Goddess!" he chanted, "Deliver us from harm. Send rain to our fields. Take sickness and plagues from us. Give our children health and strength." He prayed to the eternal Mother who had taken possession of my father's body and at the end of the prayer, a goat was killed to her. As the knife fell upon its neck and the blood flowed upon the earth, the drums pounded out, fierce and savage. After that the dance went on till the dawn broke, and at dawn Mariamma tore out of my father's body screaming and caused him to fall down in a faint, frothing at the mouth, his limbs twitching. The drumming ceased then and the drummers put away their drums, and prepared to turn homeward. And after a while his twitching ceased, and my father lay like one dead. When the sun came up high in the sky my father's body stirred and his eyes began to blink. He knew nothing at all of what had happened in the night. For the service he had given to the shrine they paid him with the meat of the goat sacrificed to the Goddess and ten rupees. That was a princely sum. For days afterwards he came home full of toddy, reeling and staggering as he sang his drunken songs in the untouchables' quarter.

He engaged again in his noisy brawls and when he entered our hut we huddled away in a corner, for we knew how he would belabour our mother, raining his blows upon her until her skin was black with his beating hand.

Such was my father and I remember him now as the men dance to Kittu. He looms large in the memories of my childhood.

He was a giant in size. My brothers hated and feared him. There were times when I too shared their hatred, and felt that I could kill him with my bare hands. But the feeling never remained. When I was very small I thought he was some kind of god, and even when I grew up I continued to be awed by the strength contained in his body, and excited by its power and rhythm and grace. Today as I remember, I realise that within that splendid framework of flesh and bone that I so greatly admired, there was only a pitiful creature, bewildered, confused, driven hither and thither by circumstances and chance like a reed in a river. It was only outwardly that he was like a tiger, but inside him was fear and confusion. He spent his fury upon his wife and children. While his children were babies, he was tender and gentle with them, but when that stage was passed and they began to walk and talk, to remember and understand, then he had nothing for them but anger and bitterness and they in their turn crouched out of his sight and had nothing in their hearts for him but fear and hatred.

So he lived out his days seeking release in toddy. In the toddy shop, caste walls fell away and he sat with many others drinking the foaming liquor until the fumes which caused reality to dissolve like mist enveloped his brain.

For my father, liquor meant happiness and heaven in a cloud of forgetfulness. And for liquor he must have money. So the thought of money hammered his mind. "Money, I must have more money!" He reeled home to get it, and there in the hut he saw us all—his wife, his children—with our hungry mouths, who stood between him and his heaven. His anger used to rise at the sight of us, and in his anger he beat his wife and children, and especially Boda.

Hunger walked with us through the days of our life. It ruled our thoughts and actions. Through sleeping and waking, from birth to death it was the thread that held the days of our life together. There was no escape from it, save in death. We were like rats running round and round in the trap of never-ending hunger. The eyes of my little brothers and sisters glistened with want. With their large heads, their swollen bellies and their spindly limbs they looked like strange insects rather than human creatures. My mother fed them on rice gruel and chilli and garlic sauce, scraping the bottom of the earthenware pot, and they gobbled up what they were given with the greed of starving animals, licking the last traces of food from their fingers. I saw this sight every day, but could not get used to it. It shamed me to see my brothers, it hurt me, I do not know why it hurt me, for the other people seemed not to mind these things at all. They went about their duty without the need to cry out or question it all. But it shamed me. And in my brother Boda it brought forth a fierce anger: as on the day when we were standing on the edge of the back lane. We were waiting while our mother worked in the latrines, emptying the buckets of their filth. My younger brothers were standing around me, and Nagi my sister was astride my hip. Boda stood a little way apart, as always, away from us.

A high-caste woman came walking down the street leading her little boy by the hand. We moved instinctively closer as if in an effort to make ourselves small enough to be almost invisible. It was strange that a high-caste woman should at this hour be walking in the street; it was the hour when the untouchables would be cleaning the latrines. But she was there and there was nothing we could do but hope that the heavens would be merciful and avert calamity. Already she was approaching us and was within a few feet of us; and I remember how I wished our physical forms would cease to be and our very shadows would be erased and would vanish. Else the terrible sin of pollution would be on our heads!

The boy was sucking a piece of sticky boiled jaggery. Its brown syrup was trickling down his elbow. I saw how the eyes of my brothers and sister fixed themselves on that sugar piece. I saw their throats move with the saliva and how they swallowed it in great gulps. Their eyes grew wide and almost leaped out of their sockets.

The lady came by. "Stay near me!" she called out warningly to her son. "The untouchables are out. Stay by me."

Who knows what childish spirit of mischief possessed the child at that moment? He gave a trill of laughter and began to tease his mother.

"I will touch them!" he shouted. "I will touch them and see what will happen!"

And he pranced around her like a young goat and advanced towards us, his eyes shining with mischief. He put out a finger: "I'll touch," he threatened. "I'll touch—"

The woman screamed. "Come back, come back at once!"

"I'll touch," the boy laughed again. "I'll touch the untouchables and what will you do then? If you beat me for that, then you will yourself be polluted!"

A shiver of dread went down my back. I knew I must not let this happen. The greatest portion of the sin would be ours if we polluted the pure. My voice which I could scarcely recognise as my own, broke from my throat:

"Stay back, stay back, Swami," and my mother hurrying to my side joined me, crying with me. "Stay away, stay away, Swami. We are cleaners of human filth, we are untouchable. Our touch is unclean; our shadows bring pollution. O our protector, I entreat you, I fall at your feet to stay away."

At the sound of my mother's voice the boy stopped. His laughter ceased abruptly. The mischief went out of his eyes and fear took its place. The thought came to him of the dreadful and unknown consequences of his disobedience.

He turned and fled and he hid his face in his mother's sari. My mother breathed with sudden relief; with deep gratitude she whispered the name of Mariamma, for a grave sin had by the Goddess' grace been averted.

But my brothers' eyes saw nothing of these things. My brothers' eyes stared unblinking at the sugar stick. The boy's mother felt a great relief. But with her relief also came her wrath that this should have happened at all.

She began to pour out abuse at us. When she saw my brothers staring at the sticky sugar, she began to scream out again: "Oh you scavenger untouchables—you whose shadows are unclean! When will you finish with your craving for other people's foods? When will you stop staring with those desire-poisoned eyes? They bulge out of their sockets until they are about to fall out!" She snatched the sugar from her son's hand and flung it into the dust. "Take it and eat," she said as she walked away with her son clutching her hand and looking back fearfully at us. "Your unclean eyes of desire have tainted it, and it would bring illness upon my child to eat unclean food."

My brothers and sister never heard her. They had picked up the tit-bit from the dust and had already begun to suck upon it, as they passed it from one to the other. My mother shaking her head and wringing her hands, returned to her interrupted work. But my brother Boda's eyes blazed with anger. He shot a look of terrible scorn at the children and then he turned away. He would not be one of us.

And I was torn by different emotions, and conflicting thoughts. There was pity in me for the little ones, but there was also shame. The anger of the caste woman seemed natural and right. But why did I feel the resentment trembling inside me? Such things were heaven-ordained, were they not? And yet a nagging doubt persisted and refused to let me be. And beneath the doubts and the humility, the resentment and the shame, there was still, I think, the endless patience which was my people's. It was in my blood as it was in the blood of my mother and her mother's before her. From destiny and one's karma I knew there was no escape; and yet insistently something cried out inside me that there must somewhere, in this life, be a miracle that would redeem us, set us free, make us human as others were human, and not the creatures that now we were, of a dim twilight existence, neither wholly animal nor wholly man. Somewhere there must be a meaning to this parched routine of birth and toil, hunger, death and rebirth. Nothing would stifle this voice inside me.

But there were days that were different; like the days of Mariamma's festivals; and there were the days when the Great Feeding of the Untouchable came round once a month, on the day of the moonless night at the Venugopalapuram temple. On that day the torture of our hunger was held back for a while and our stomachs were cooled. Hundreds of scavenger folk swarmed to the temple backlane for on that day the banana leaves off which the caste people had eaten, with the remains of food upon them, as well as the left-overs in the big temple vessels were thrown to them. We too went, my parents, my brothers and sister and I, along with the hundreds who came from villages as far as ten and fifteen miles away.

"By the grace and mercy of Venugopala we shall eat today and fill our hungry bellies," our people said to each other, as they hurried along crossing their hands at the wrists and tapping their fingers fervently on their cheeks.

It is said that the custom of feeding the untouchables has been there as long as the temple has existed with its sculptured gopurams and its seven holy tanks. And the temple is old, though not as old as the shrine of Mariamma. Venugopala compared with the rock Goddess, is only a child—a mere babe in arms. And yet the main temple where the Deity stands has existed for hundreds of years; the gopurams with their bright-coloured sculptured gods and goddesses came later. These were built, they say, when men grew evil and took to thieving and looting. That was also the time when it became necessary to erect barriers to keep out the untouchable folk. I can see the temple gopuram now from where I sit. It is around this temple that all my destiny has been woven. And the story of the temple has become my story and Kittu's—my son's. I remember how when I was young we saw the people go in and out of this same Venugopala's temple and we heard the music that woke the god, that played as he went about his daily tasks, and when he was being rocked to sleep at night. We heard from our distance the jangle of the temple bells. From our distance we too bowed to the Lord, to Venugopala the Flute Player and prayed to him. He stood in the deepest heart of the temple, as he stands today, inside its cool and tranquil blackness, and we who are untouchable had never in those days seen the idol with our eyes, but in our hearts we knew him. We knew his ageless beauty; we knew that there was a smile on the Flute Player's lips which had magic in it. It was said that if seen too clearly in the light, that smile would make such tumult in men's hearts that they would leave all earthly things without a thought and go seeking after its mystery. That is why the idol stood in the dark with only the dim yellow light of the wick lamps flickering on it.

In bygone ages, they said, a man had seen this idol in a dream, lying beneath a rock in the river bed. Then in the same dream he had heard voices around him, ordering him to go and dig for it in the river bed. He wanted to obey the voices, but he put it off, for there were other things to do. And also he felt a reluctance to chase what was after all only a dream. But the voices would not let him be and at last one day he could no longer resist them, and he left everything and went walking on the lonely path until he came to the spot in the river bed.

He began to dig in this spot going deeper and deeper until his pickaxe hit a great rock, and try as he might, he could go no further. He sat down, tired and dispirited, thinking what a fool he had been after all.

But as he sat there cursing himself, he heard the sound of music. Its sweetness crept through his body, and flowed into his blood. It filled his entire being. Drawn by a stranger power, not his own, he felt his hand grasp the pickaxe once more. He bent down to dig again. And at the first blow the rock cracked and opened and there within it lay the idol of Venugopala, the cowherd boy with the flute.

After that news of the appearance of the idol spread. People flocked to see it. The king ordered the building of the mighty temple by the master builders in the land. That was hundreds of years ago, and the site was marked by the gods when seven holy springs gushed out of the earth. They were the rivers Ganga, Jumna, Saraswati, Godavari, Krishna, Kavery and our own mother, the beautiful Vasumati, and they all came to do homage to the Flute Player God. These seven springs feed the seven holy tanks of the temple where the caste folk went to wash and purify themselves before they entered into the presence of the Deity. They say there is nothing in all the world to rival the beauty of that image, nothing to compare with the carving on its stone columns and walls. From afar you can see the domes of the temple gleaming in the sunlight and we too, though untouchable, were privileged to see with our' own eyes the gods and goddesses that adorned the outer gopurams. And we could see too the branches and leaves of the mighty peepul in the outer yard. It was said that the peepul had been there since the temple began. Perhaps it was a sapling then, pushing its way out of the earth at the call of rain and sun. It stood there then, as it still does, magnificent and massive, with its branches outspreading in all directions. Hordes of monkeys swing among them as they have always done; generations of birds and squirrels nest amidst its foliage; and in the hollows of its great trunk still sleep jewelled snakes that guard the temple treasure. Creepers climb sinuously up its gigantic body and cling to it; in the fullness of their time they fall away and die and their young ones spring up, twisting their way skywards; and that is why it is said that this peepul is not a tree at all but, in reality, a mighty rishi who stands deep in meditation, lost in the realization of God: for whoever heard of a tree feeding creepers with its blood and continuing to live as this one does? It is the peepul to which they tied my Kittu before they set fire to him and sent him to his death. He screamed and cried out for mercy, but they had none. He had transgressed. So they sent him to his death. He went in to see the Flute Player's image, he who was untouchable. So they poured kerosene oil upon him and set fire to his clothes and they sent him to his death.

In the days when I was young there were many stories told about the temple and the black deity inside it, and we, though we were untouchable and might not enter the temple, heard them too and knew them. Often, late in the evening, we sat around Kantanna and he spoke to us of many things. Kantanna had wisdom and experience, and could tell a story in a living voice.

When the stars came out and the smoke of the cooking

fires hung thick and low, Kantanna sat outside his hut and we hurried to be with him and listen.

He told us the story of the thief who crept into the temple at dead of night to steal the jewellery upon the idol. The thief was a wicked man and had committed many crimes, but when he put his hand upon Venugopala, he heard the flute play, and the melody flooded over his spirit. It filled his ears and his entire being, and that was how he came suddenly to lose his sanity and reason. He went mad after that and lived in the temple, his clothes in tatters, laughing and weeping by turns and eating the scraps that were thrown to him out of pity. There were other stories: there was the story of Kanaka who was untouchable like us and the saint whose heart was filled with the love of God. This Kanaka sang songs of his making and yearned for a glimpse of the deity in the temple, but they drove him away with sticks and stones to the back of the temple, because he was untouchable and lowly. So there he went and he stood still singing. But when the priests went in to perform the great puja, why, that day, a wonderful thing had happened! The stone image itself had turned, and now had its back to them, while its face looked out from the back window to the lane where Kanaka stood singing the holy name!

And the story too of Champaka, the courtesan of Venugopalapuram. She had lived, said Kantanna, in the days gone by, and to this day she remained alive. She sat beneath the stones of the Venugopala temple—and so would she remain for ever and ever, one with God, and freed from the chains of birth and rebirth. In her days Venugopalapuram used to be a great and busy city, capital of the kingdom and full of marvellous sights—wide streets and busy market places, gardens and houses of pleasure where women famed for their beauty and their skill in music and dance, lived and entertained.

Champaka was one such. She was so beautiful that kings and chieftains, nobles and priests all came to her, travelling long distances to lay priceless gifts at her feet. Champaka received them graciously. As time passed her wealth grew and so did her renown. The fame of her learning spread. Kings discussed matters of state with her and in her hands she held the fate of many a kingdom and empire.

But when her glory was at its height there came to her doorstep a wandering beggar singing the name of God and strumming on his one-stringed lute. And when she heard his songs, she grew strangely silent and thoughtful. And when he had bidden her goodbye and left her she felt a loneliness staring at her and looking into her heart. The loneliness would not leave her, and she grew restless with it. Doubts began to rack her spirit, and shadows began to appear under her eyes because she could not sleep for long hours in the night. Then after a while an endless yearning possessed her.

"What is the matter?" asked the people who visited her. "What has happened to her laughter and happiness? It isn't the same as it used to be." She was young and talented as ever—but she was not the same. She wandered away from her mansion, dressed in white and wearing no ornaments except her beads of prayer, and she gave no reason for her behaviour when they asked her, but only turned her face away. "Why?" they asked, "She is young still and beautiful and desirable, and there are princes and noblemen ready to die at a word from her." After a while she did not sing or dance any more and her guests stopped coming to her, because she had nothing now to offer them for their pleasure. The servants in the house, seeing their mistress in a dream, ate up her wealth or carried it away. And what remained Champaka herself took and gave and gave to the poor till there was nothing left. It did not matter to her that she was uncared for now and alone—nor that her wealth and possessions had all gone. The things of the world no longer mattered. She sat alone in her rooms, and no one knew that she was performing penance, praying and meditating alone, deep in the night.

One day the townsfolk saw her walking towards the temple—empty-handed now, because she had no offerings of jewels or gold coins or silks or brocades: she had only a garland of flowers for the Deity. When men saw her (the same men who had visited her often in the days when she was rich), they spat on her and called out abuse and insults. An angry crowd followed her, but Champaka saw nothing. She was singing the names of God. Her feet took her forward. As she reached the temple doors, they picked up stones and began to fling them at her. But Champaka's eyes saw only the Deity and her lips sang only the name of God. It was then that the Deity of the temple worked his miracle. The stones, they say, changed to flowers as they fell on her and at her feet—here in our own Venugopala temple, here in our town of Venugopalapuram. But Champaka did not see what happened, for her eyes were closed and her mind was on the Lord.

She was climbing the stone steps when they cried out: "Bar the doors—she is a sinner!" They shut the doors on her face and Champaka stood outside singing the thousand names of God, and the priests and the rich and the powerful men of the realm stood inside. And it was then that the second miracle took place. For each name that she uttered the temple echoed to the rafters in answer: "Champaka! Champaka! Champaka!" Each stone, each brick, each hinge upon the door cried out "Champaka"; the flames in the sacred lamps repeated her name; the little stone images of the thirty-three crores of Gods in the temple pillars and walls sang it out. Then the bells began to to clang of their own accord, the drums to throb, the conch shells blew, and they too called the name. And from the Golden Flute there poured out a thousand melodies. Wherever the priests turned, "Champaka" sounded in their ears, rising on all sides and swelling like a storm, till it seemed to them that they were going mad. They flung the doors open and fled, crazed with fear, and that day they performed no worship. Then the next day, gathering courage in their hands they returned, trembling, to the temple.

As they came they saw Champaka at the door, where they had left her. She sat in the lotus posture, and her eyes were closed, her lips were smiling. She did not breathe. And then they knew that she had become one with the Lord—that she had entered into the eternal meditation where she sat, and was freed for ever and ever from the burden of birth and rebirth. Then over the frame of her body they built her tomb of stone and the temple was silent once more as if nothing had ever happened.

All these stories we heard from Kantanna, the story teller. They were stories that had grown around our own Venugopala temple. We listened to Kantanna attentively and from afar we watched the worshippers going into the temple. From afar, we too joined our hands in worship.... and never did it occur to us that we could be among the worshippers; that we could stand before the Deity and worship as they did. Our place was outside. We may not approach the Deity except in our hearts. And yet, said Kantanna, though we may not approach him, *He* would not forsake us. He would come to us and be with us. For He was God and God cannot be defiled, as uncooked rice or flowers or naked children cannot be defiled. In the old days this explanation satisfied the people—all except Boda and Soma. I looked at my brothers furtively, and I saw Boda's eyes were angry and sneering. And I saw Soma get up and walk away with a mocking laugh. As she did so, she threw a glance at me and I knew she was thinking me a weakling and a fool. But I would not go with her. Instead I sat there with the others. My eyes glanced curiously at the faces of my companions. Impassive faces, glazed eyes; they asked for no more than this vague blessing that Venugopala visit them in their homes, and they were very satisfied. I felt doubts clamour inside me, and "Fool," said Soma in my ear, "Kantanna has an easy tongue, and you have the brain of a goat...."

But I sat there mutely and could not bring myself to go with her. I believed in miracles in those days; I believed in rewards for good deeds done and I could not shed my faith. Soma called me a fool. But I could not help being what I was, and unable to answer her back and unsure of myself, I hung my head and remained silent.

On the day of the Poor Feeding we squatted in groups, waiting. My stomach rumbled and my mouth watered as the smell of the food reached my nostrils. My brothers whimpered in their usual way, and my mother sat rocking the baby in her arms, and murmuring Mariamma's name. Late in the afternoon there was a shout and the temple servants came out carrying the buckets full of banana leaves with food which people had left upon them. The scramble started then. Everyone sprang to their feet and began to push and jostle, to call and shout, clamouring to get a share. I saw my father striding up, pushing down all who came in his path. The Junior Priest came to supervise over the throwing of the banana leaves. He called out for order, shouting to us terms of abuse and obscenity, leering and showing his yellow teeth as the servants began to fling the leaves into our midst. "Stand back, stand back," he shouted, "what! will you defile me, a priest of the temple?"

We moved back, at his word but our eyes and all our thoughts continued to be fixed on the food that would cool our bellies on that blessed day. Soma, swinging her hips and tossing her head, made her way to the very front where she stood laughing and talking. She did not lower her eyes, or bend her head. She had no fear of anyone and she looked at the Junior Priest in the face and called out for her share. The priest's face contorted. He grew very abusive. But his anger only made Soma laugh, and swagger about more. "Throw me food, great master," Soma trilled: "Throw me a large portion. The largest you have."

None of the others said a word. They cast looks of disapproval and anger at her. They did not like the Junior Priest, but they did not approve of Soma's brazen ways either. But what did she care? She scarcely noticed them as they moved to let her pass. The priest ordered food to be thrown to her and she laughed and made her way back through the crowd, swinging her hips and tossing her head. When she had gone the jostling and the clamouring started again. I felt the desire in my belly grow bigger. I heard old Granny Ponchu call out: "Don't stand there as if you were a mass of dung. Do you think that food will fall of its own accord into your open mouths? Fools, you must fight and push and struggle if you want a share."

But my mother was too gentle and timid to do as Ponchu said. We waited and my stomach rumbled and my brothers began to cry out aloud. It seemed to me that we would never get any food—that we would stand there waiting for all eternity, and we would remain hungry. But after a while the Junior Priest's eyes would fall on us. And he would bare his teeth into a smile. When he smiled he looked like a jackal. "Come, girl, come," the Junior Priest would say. "Come for your share. Are you not hungry?" My mother would give me a little push then, and whisper encouragement in my ear. But I hung back. My feet would not move. A fear clutched my heart at the sound of his voice and at the sight of those leering yellow teeth, and those jackal eyes. "Go, child!" my mother would whisper. Smiling still, the Junior Priest threw the banana leaves of food to me. "Here, catch this, slut," but in my confusion I let several fall into the dust. And the Junior Priest shrieked with laughter to see that. My mother and my brothers collected the food together: "Mariamma has been merciful," whispered my mother. "And Venugopala has given us food! Come, let us eat." We would squat around her, and my brothers could scarce keep from trembling in their impatience, while she portioned out the food with great deliberation and ceremony.

Our hearts were full of gratitude and the name of Venugopala was constantly on our tongues. We thanked him for his goodness and mercy, for the leavings that were thrown to us. "What should we do if it was not for Venugopala's mercy?" For a while our hunger was forgotten as we made our way back to our quarters. Then the dreary round began again.

The Temple Feeding receded from our memory after a day or two. Once again we were at the mercy of our hunger.

That was when I was young. When I grew and was

married the same order continued. Kittu and Mada and I went every month with the other untouchable folk to get the leavings from the Temple Feast.

"I will not eat leavings," said Kittu one day. He was ten years old then, and his eyes were defiant as Boda's used to be.

"You will when your belly is tortured with hunger," old Ponchu croaked. "You will eat dirt and mud if you are hungry."

"I will not." He began to sob and cry and Mada gathered him in his arms and soothed him with gentle words until he fell asleep. He slept that day, and did not eat, for he would not eat leavings. O my son Kittu... he will never weep or laugh or be angry again, my Kittu who was named for the Deity in the temple. There never will be heard any more the sound of his young and laughing voice. He screamed and screamed in agony—they said—as the flames consumed him, and now he is under the earth, a corpse, a dreadful, fearful, unrecognisable thing.

"How like Boda he is!" everybody said. In a way they were right. But not completely. They looked alike—the same long head and the same curly kinky hair, and dark skin, the same broad forehead, the same sullen lip and sharp chin. Outwardly they were alike perhaps, in feature and limb. But Kittu was full of laughter and talk, Boda spoke little. In Boda's eyes was a secret smouldering anger. The children were afraid of Boda. He had nothing to say to them. Sometimes he brought them parched rice or gram, but they slunk away at his approach, remembering the many times when he beat them and kicked them and twisted their ears.

There was a springhead of anger and bitterness in my brother's heart, and it poisoned the food he ate and the very air he breathed. There was an anger in him, such an anger as I have never seen, save in a man of caste who was defiled. Though my mother loved him above all of us (we could not help realising that), between him and my father there was nothing but a stony coldness. As time passed, the distance between them gaped wider and wider. The silences that separated them widened into great chasms of bitterness. Something in Boda's face and eyes caused my father to turn from him, and brought from his lips a torrent of vile and angry abuse. One day their quarrel came to a head. I must have been seven years old at the time. But Boda was nearly a man. My mother was doling out our portions of cold rice to us. She was pouring out the red sauce of ground chillies and garlic on the rice. My brothers fell on their food. When they held out the earthenware bowl for more, my mother scraped the bottom of the pot for the grains left in it. The children were not satisfied. They whimpered and cried for more. They knew that in another pot my mother always hid away a portion of rice for my father to eat, when he came from the drink shop. Sometimes he ate it at midnight, sometimes the next day on waking from his drunken sleep. The children's eyes, their thoughts, their desire, were on that food.

My mother would not touch my father's portion. She fed the children from out of her own bowl and sometimes I slipped in a morsel or two from mine, but their restless eyes continued to wander to the other pot. Puttu began to complain querulously. Nagi, the girl, began to cry. One by one the children took up the cry. Presently they were all wailing together and Boda could not stand the din. He did not like the children to make a noise. He shouted:

"Shut them up—strangle them—stuff rice into their mouths and down their throats—" The children's wails subsided at the sound of his voice but only for a few minutes and presently they began to whimper again, casting glances at Boda.

"There is rice in the other bowl," Boda glowered at my mother. "Why don't you feed it to them, and let us have some peace?"

The children stared at Boda, open-mouthed. Their whimpering stopped suddenly with gulping noises. "Is he mad?" I thought. My mother gave Boda a silent, sidelong look but she said nothing. She sat as if paralysed. I began to collect the children's bowls. Boda moved towards us from the corner where he was sitting. "Why don't you feed them?" he addressed our mother again, "Can't you see they are hungry?"

My brothers' eyes began to shine. My mother looked up startled, terror in her face. Boda took a step towards the rice-pot in the corner, bent and scooped out rice in his hand.

"Come, take this. Eat—eat—eat!"

"Father!" One of the children whispered fearfully.

"Huh!" Boda scoffed: "Father! Your father only feels thirst—no hunger. What does he want with rice? Rice is for the hungry, but your father's food is toddy, and toddy he will have even if he has to make it with your blood. Why must he have rice as well? Tell me why?"

Just as he was talking, my father came reeling in, very drunk but his wits still about him. He looked at Boda, dipping into his rice-pot and his face darkened. His words came out thickly: "My rice—my rice—do you dare to touch my rice?"

"O Boda," my mother whispered: "Boda, do not anger him—do not make him angry—" She put her hand out to touch his shoulder, but he shook it away with such a violent gesture that my mother started back in distress and fear. I was praying to Mariamma in my heart and my limbs were cold and my lips stiff with fear. My father's reeling figure loomed at the entrance, his eyes were bloodshot and his breath reeking of toddy. He was talking incoherently, pointing his unsteady forefinger at Boda.

"You have given me a name, have you not?" Boda said, "Use that to address me by."

Huh—" sneered my father. "He answers back. The son of a bitch—his tongue has grown very strong—the food in his stomach has done it—" Then he turned to my mother—"Your son, woman—your son! He has a hole for a stomach and he will not work—no, he will not soil his hands with work."

Boda had heard stronger language from my father than this. He had been used to far worse—his ears had been cuffed and his nose punched, but for some reason it was today he hit out. Suddenly, in a flash Boda faced my father, baring his teeth and glowering— "You dare—you dare—you shiftless scoundrel—you babbler, liar—"

But my father never heard him at all. He had lurched forward and begun to hit out at Boda, reeling about the room, shouting abuse. And then suddenly without warning, as the children ran about in fear, he was advancing upon Boda. I cried out—and I heard my mother's scream, and the terrified voices of the children. Suddenly the place was full of people. The neighbours had come hearing us. And Ponchu was shouting, "Are you mad —what are you doing? Killing your son?" My father was beating Boda and he was like a man possessed.

"Son—son," he was shouting back, "No son of mine, that one. And I will kill him, yes, kill him before he destroys me. He will not soil his hands with work, the pig, and he will eat." He was completely out of his senses. I think he would have killed my brother, if the neighbours had not held him back. Others held back Boda, who was standing with his hands on his hips, insolent, defying, daring the drunken man.

In the end my father went out of the house. It was past midnight when the neighbours left us, talking, discussing, debating in loud voices, and then we lay down, my mother, the children, Boda and I, and we were silent until morning. I lay on the floor and wondered about the tumult in Boda's mind. And I prayed to Mariamma to forgive us all for our sins and to bless us and give us rice. And especially to bless Boda.

From the next day on after that Boda began to work. Silently, with set face he began to lift the buckets that our mother put down and to bear them away. He spoke rarely. One day our mother suggested that he sweep the drains of the Hanumanapura lane as the sweeper of that locality had fallen ill and was vomiting black blood. They did not think the sweeper would live for many days. Boda took up the work and began to earn his rice. He brought his earnings home to our mother and gave them to her when our father was not about, and then he would turn away sullenly from her pleasure-filled eyes.

But Kittu, my son, was not like Boda : Kittu was a joyous child. He was born in the year of our Independence and his dawning eyes had been blessed with the sight of our flag rising to the sky, proclaiming us a brave people, free to shape their destiny. He was loved—Mada fed him with his hands, cradled him in his arms, let him ride upon his back and shoulders, and sent him to school.

"He must go to school," Mada said. "Our Kittu must have learning. Then he will grow up the equal of all men, and no man's slave. That is what the law of the land says, does it not, Lakshmi?"

Children of God

So when Kittu was five years old Mada bought for him a shirt and knee length trousers and brown cloth shoes. He bought him a cap and slate and pencil, and made me find the printed alphabet book that Father Pierre had given me, and which I had kept carefully by, wrapped up in cloth with neem leaves to keep it from cockroaches and insects. He led his son by the hand and took him to the Panchayat school, and I went with them, because I was eager to see our Kittu enter the temple of learning, and also because Mada felt that I might be able to speak and explain since I too had gone to school and learned to read and write. The neighbours stood on the road to watch as we went and to call out to us, wishing us well and giving Kittu their blessing. As we reached the school-house I felt my spirits leap and dance with joy and expectation.

"I am afraid," Mada whispered to me, and I felt Kittu's fingers tighten on mine, and all three of us hesitated; our steps faltered and we halted and looked at each other, unsure of the course we must take. Mada's eyes were staring at me and I could see the fear in them. Kittu lifted his head and turned his gaze at his father. He moved close to me and when I put my arm around him he turned to look at me for comfort.

"Would it be wise?" Mada's eyes seemed to be saying. "Are you sure all will be well?"

"All will be well," I said to him aloud. "Why should it not be? Now we are untouchable no more. We are an Independent people. It is Rama Rajya now, and in Rama Rajya we are not untouchable."

"Will you speak to the teachers?" Mada asked, moistening his lips nervously with his tongue.

"No, you speak," I answered him. "It is better for a man to speak, and I will add my voice to yours."

"But you have been to a school," Mada protested, "you are learned which I am not, Lakshmi. You know how to read and write...."

"We will both speak." I compromised. "We will stand thus...." I arranged our little family in the position in which we would meet the teacher in the school-house—Mada first, holding Kittu by the hand and myself behind them both.

Kittu jumped up and laughed, eager to start. But Mada restrained him and told him that this was no childish matter. It was a grave step in a person's life and Kittu should be quiet and serious and stand respectfully and speak respectfully, and learn all they would teach him and become a learned man. That subdued Kittu and he became solemn and serious again. So we went to the school-house.

But the news of our approach had already gone before us. News travels fast in a place like ours. As we neared the school-house we saw the hostile faces of the people standing in groups on the street, and I felt the palms of my hands grow clammy with sweat.

"There is nothing to fear," I whispered to Mada. "The law is on our side." He did not answer; but his lips were moving. I think he was repeating the name of Mariamma, begging her protection as I was. There was a crowd at the school-house—a tight little knot of people who stood as if they had known of our coming and were waiting for us. But the school-teacher who was a frightened looking, mouse-like man spoke mildly:

"How will school benefit your son?" he said. "How will reading and writing help to fill the belly? A man needs to follow in his father's profession."

I said: "Master, we fall at your feet. We have but one child, one son, and we have wished that he should learn to read and write."

Children of God

"You have learnt these foolish thoughts from the foreign missionaries," the school-teacher cut in. "The missionaries have spoilt you and your tribe." We answered nothing to that. The silence that followed was hot with the anger of the group of people who stood watching and waiting.

Mada bent low and touched the ground and I did the same. "The boy longs to learn, master." Mada said, "He longs to go to school."

"A school for scavengers!" now it was one of the other people who spoke, and I recognised the jeering voice of the oil-seller's son. He had pushed himself out from the crowd and he stood before us with his hands on his hips. His small spider's eyes were full of hate.

"Go from here, scavengers, untouchables. This is no place for you."

"The law—" Soma's voice answered him. She had come behind us and was standing with me now. "There is a law today that can punish you if you call a person untouchable or refuse to allow him to enter school or temple."

"Law...law...what do you know of the law?" sneered the oil-seller's son.

"As much as concerns us, whom you call untouchables." Soma answered, as insolent as ever. "The law of the land protects us."

"Ha!" said another in a voice heavy with scorn.

"A law that has been set down by an untouchable himself."

"What do you expect?"

A portly gentleman in a pink turban and gold earrings spoke up: "Laws—you talk of law. What do you understand? The only laws that have any authority are those that were made by the ancients!" He wagged his forefinger at us. "They are God-given laws! Do you understand? That is why they are laws. They may not change at the will and pleasure of mortal creatures, as the so-called laws of today do." He came nearer and stood on the steps of the school-house. His voice grew lower, smoother, his eyes grew cunning. "Go, good folk... and do not defy heaven. What will you get by doing that?" Mada turned to me, and our eyes met. And then I saw Kittu's face turned up also towards us. He was looking at us anxiously, not understanding anything.

"Let us go back," Mada whispered, and I felt my gorge rise.

"You could be jailed for this, master," I uttered, speaking to the teacher, though I do not know how I had the courage to say it. "There could be trouble...." I saw their eyes move uneasily; with swift glances they were consulting each other, suddenly realising that the ground on which they had stood had shifted and things were not as they used to be.

"Yes, there could be trouble if we carried this too far," their eyes seemed to say. And so they made a compromise, not wishing to lose face and yet not willing to take the risk of defying the new law. They declared that Kittu could come to the school-house, but he must sit outside the door, removed from the other boys. And on the days that important Government people came from outside to tour the district, then Kittu was to stay away altogether. We looked at each other, Mada and Kittu and I. In the end it was I who decided at last that Kittu should be sent to school on these terms. There was a nagging doubt in my mind about the rightness of it. "There is a law against it." I murmured to Ponchu, when we returned to our quarters. But Ponchu answered, in her usual way: "What can a law do? Can it change an untouchable into a priest of God? A man's caste is the result of his birth, and his birth is the result of past lives, past sins and past good deeds." Some of our people said to me, "You are nothing but a worm...." The thought of Kittu sitting far from the other children, sitting alone outside the door, made my heart heavy. The poor teacher said: "I will see what I can do," struggling with himself and his fears. "I will see." And during the days that followed he closed his eyes to Kittu's stealthy advance into the room where the others sat. First Kittu moved nearer the door. Then he put his finger on the threshold; then one day he crossed into the room; then he inched his way across the floor until he was within a foot or two from the other children. And that was the day when the elders of the village and parents of the children came to the school-house and beat the child Kittu and sent him crying home.

"You must not enter the school-room," they told Kittu, "The next time worse may happen. There may be a riot, and you will find your head broken and your stomach ripped open."

"But there is a law against untouchability! The Government of free India." I persisted when Kittu had told us the story in his childish words.

"Woman," they replied. "What do you know of law and Government? Hold your tongue or it will be bad for you...." And Mada said to me later: "Let us be thankful for what we have got. If we reach out to grasp heaven we may lose earth as well."

The earth has covered Kittu's body at last. My son has gone from me. He will never return, no matter what laws are passed or what cases are won. No matter what punishment is visited on the people who caused his death, my brave, handsome Kittu, my jewel, my golden boy will never come back to me.

In the days before Kittu was born also there were brawls in the streets sometimes. And once there was a case in the court. It concerned Boda, my brother. We were standing one day on the edge of the street while our mother was working. Boda as always stood a little way apart from us. I held Nagi on my hip. The others played in the dust. A youth sauntered down the road. There were diamonds in his ears and gold rings on his fingers as befitted his station in life, for his father owned the toddy shops and farmed them out on contracts. The boy sauntered idly down the road. He would not normally, I think, have noticed us but for the way in which Boda stood. Boda did not stand as an untouchable scavenger was expected to stand: he did not hang his head, or drop his eyes, or clasp his hands and beg to be forgiven. Boda looked the youth in the face. I too saw how Boda looked the youth in the face and fear clutched at my heart. The youth stopped. He stared at us and then his eyes moved up and down Boda's frame. On the corner of Boda's mouth was a smile. I was wishing I could wipe it away. "Boda must not smile. Boda must not smile like that." I thought, and hoped—with all my heart I hoped—that there would be no trouble.

The youth snarled at us:

"Untouchables, why do you stand upon the public street defiling all who come and go?" he said.

"Oh my father and my mother—" I began.

But Boda moved quickly towards me and pushed me aside.

"We will stand where we choose!" he answered. "This road does not belong to you, does it, nor to your father?"

"You answer me back?" the other shouted. "Pigs—carriers of filth—you make bold to answer me!"

My mother came to the spot panting and breathless. "I fall at your feet, my father, my mother. I worship the ground you tread. Forgive him, forgive us!" She began to cry.

Boda sprang up between them. "Questions require answers, do they not?" He was addressing the boy directly. "You asked me a question, did you not?"

"Be quiet, be quiet, my brother," I said, "You must not—"

"Be quiet yourself!" my brother snapped angrily. "Why should I be quiet? God has given me a tongue, has he not? Is that tongue not for use?" He pushed me aside roughly and faced the boy again. "This is a public road," he went on, "It is not your father's road, is it? Nor your mother's lover's inherited property? Anyone may use it and you cannot forbid us." The youth drew in his breath sharply. Then from out of his mouth there spilled such a volley of abuse that it made my blood run cold to hear it.

"Take care," Boda warned. His eyes were flashing, his mouth working. "Mind how you talk!"

"Huh!" snorted the boy. "You-untouchables-cleaners of latrines you-"

At that moment the stone hit me. I had seen the youth pick it up. It came flying now and hit me on the cheek below my eyes. I reeled. There was a red blot on Nagi's skirt and I saw it was blood.

I heard my mother scream; I saw my brothers cling to each other and stare in terror. Boda was breathing hard through his dilated nostrils. His lips were parted to show his teeth; his fists were clenching and unclenching. With a yell Boda charged at the boy and he began to rain blows upon him. "Take that!" Boda screamed. "Take that, you—you foul-mouthed liar. Take that for yourself and that for your father. Go on—" he continued. "Go on and take that for the mother who bore you, and these for each of the sins you commit."

The blows rained faster and we were helpless with fear. And then I sprang upon Boda and caught him. A crowd collected. Someone held back the toddy contractor's son. But they strained towards each other, he and Boda, and there was murder in their eyes. A woman began to scream hysterically pointing to us. "It is the rice they eat that goes to their head." Another woman answered her, her voice high and shrill. "Their arrogance has gone beyond all bounds. Today they pollute our streets and tomorrow they will demand to sit with us for the temple feast. And the day after—do you know what will happen? Do you know? I will tell you—the day after tomorrow if we do not take care they will ask for our daughters! Mark my words, That's what they will do if we are not careful."

"That is what it will come to!" Many voices began to shrill together. My mother, as usual, began to cry out for forgiveness; she was on her knees knocking her head on the earth. I did not know which way to turn. It was the same pattern repeating itself over and over again.

The police came. They brandished their sticks about, the people began to run helter-skelter in all directions. The policemen talked to one or two people. Then they came to where we stood. They handcuffed Boda and led him away. The crowd stood around, muttering and talking, and people cast angry glances in our direction.

"Oh Mariamma!" my mother cried. "Deliver us from harm."

"Come, let us go," I whispered to her, helping her up. We

backed away and made our way home, and all the way home my mother wept and called out to Mariamma.

There was a case against Boda in the court room in Manur and we had to give evidence. We stood outside as far as we could, huddled round our mother. The children on our hips hid their faces in fear. After we had waited all morning my mother and I were called up. As we went in, my knees shook and turned to water and would not support me. For I had never stood under one roof with those of caste.

I called upon Mariamma to succour and protect me. They asked me questions and my voice stuck in the dryness of my throat when I tried to answer.

"Mariamma, oh Mariamma," I whispered. Then my tongue loosened and my voice began to come out. I began to answer the questions they put me though my hands were cold. I answered as well as I could all that I could remember. At the end of it all, they asked me to step down from the box. Then it was the turn of the toddy-contractor's son to speak. As I heard his answers to the questions, it began to seem to me that we had moved into a nightmare world of unreality. The boy was speaking to defend himself. He was walking down the street, he said, peaceable as he always was, looking to his own business, when the untouchable Boda had rushed upon him and begun to beat him. He had said nothing, done nothing. He was a peaceable young man, and of good caste. Why should he deign to enter into a quarrel with an untouchable?

I glanced at my mother. My whole frame was trembling as I heard him. But my mother seemed not to belong to that place at all. She was in another world, in the world of

Mariamma, and the torrent of words that issued from the boy's lips did not touch her at all. I remember thinking: "Is there no retribution? Do the gods not punish those who lie? Surely...surely...his tongue will rot, his eyes will fall out if he continues thus." But nothing happened. He continued to speak and the others continued to listen.

But somewhere, somehow, Mariamma must have heard my mother's prayer, because in the end Boda was let off. Later I heard it said that he was let off not because he was proved innocent, but because they had not enough proof to show him guilty. So we slipped out and waited in the compound, making ourselves as small as we could in the hope that we would not be seen or noticed.

After a while the people came streaming out. I can remember still how I started when I saw Boda among them. He made no attempt to cower or hide. He held his head up, and he walked as if he was one of them.

Sudden pride filled me to see him thus, a man just like all men; I prayed to Mariamma again, grateful to her that she had brought him out from the snares of wicked falsehoods that they had laid for him. But my father did not feel that way: he stared angrily at Boda and muttered curses under his breath. "This will be the end," he cried, wringing his hands desperately. "This one has brought evil into our house and life," and he struck his forehead, worried and hopeless. That night when we got home he beat Boda again. I thought a demon had possessed him, as his fists rained blows on my brother's face and head and back. I flew between them, and his fury fell upon me. The neighbours came in and again held him, and everyone was shouting and cursing. At last his anger spent itself out, and my father sank upon the floor in a fit of weeping.

It was on the morning after that night that we found that

Children of God

Boda had left us and gone. He had slipped away in the night. All day I waited for his return, but the day passed and the night passed without any sign of him. And after many days of waiting we knew without words that Boda had gone from us. No one had seen him.

"Let him go," said my father, his eyes shadowed with bitterness and hatred. "What did he do for us that we should mourn his going? He brought evil upon us and nothing but evil. Let him go." But my mother wept softy. She turned her face away and wiped the tears with the edge of her tattered sari. He was her first-born and she loved him the best.

Boda did not return... not for a long, long time. As the days passed we began to speak less and less about him. In our young minds the memory of his face grew hazy. Only my mother continued to wait and pray and hope. And I was lonely without him, I missed him at every turn.

In Venugopalapuram, the story of his fight with the toddy-contractor's son travelled swiftly from mouth to mouth, and grew limbs. And some said that Boda had run away with a high caste girl and others insisted that he had forced his way into the temple. The elders of our community met together under the mango tree and decided that as penalty our family should pay a sum of a rupee towards the shrine and sacrifice a cock to the Goddess, and my parents gladly obeyed, thankful that things were not worse. But for many days afterwards, I sensed a seething anger against us amongst the caste people. "Huh!" I heard them say, "Today they walk upon our streets, and tomorrow—where will all this lead to tomorrow? Where?" But we were used to their anger. So much had we seen in our lives that a little more or a little less made no difference. Besides there were always the kind-hearted and the merciful men and women of caste who took pity on us and threw us scraps of left-over food and torn clothes. We clasped our hands and blessed them. We marvelled at their kindness. We were grateful to them.

Sidda went too, some time after that. Sidda went another way. How old was he then? Ten? Twelve? Fourteen? He had a bloated belly and limbs like an insect's. His eyes also resembled an insect's large, frightened eyes, with an insect's cunning darting about them. On the way to Mariamma's shrine one day Sidda plucked the end of my skirt for my attention. "Come here, come away from the rest of them. There is something I have to tell you.

"What is it?" I whispered. But he drew me away:

"Not here, not with all these people around us." he whispered. When we were by ourselves Sidda said. "I am going away and I shall not come back." He began to bite his nails and weep.

"I am hungry," said Sidda. "My stomach is empty all the time. And I must work carrying human filth and be forever untouchable. I don't want that and so I am going."

"You do not want to carry filth?" I cried in astonishment, "who will do this work then if you and I do not? Aren't we scavengers? Isn't this the work for which we have been born? If we do not work how shall we eat?" I repeated all that I had heard them say.

"Eat?" exclaimed Sidda. "Did you say *eat?* It is so many days since I have had food to fill my belly. What is it we eat, Lachi, except the curses and abuses of the caste folk? I am hungry the whole time, and at night there are cramps in my stomach!" He began to rub his belly with his hands. "Oh no!" he said, "don't try to keep me. I must go." And because I did not know what to say to him, I put out my hand to touch him and caress him. But he pushed me away.

"How can you be so foolish, Sidda?" I asked him. "What are these thoughts in your mind? Where, where will you go?

What will you do? How can you escape the fate you have been born into? The karma of other lives? The good and evil you have done bring their rewards and their punishments...." I talked and talked, babbled on and on, but Sidda drummed on his bloated belly and repeated, sullenly, "All I know is that we are hungry and accursed in the present, that is all I know."

He began to weep, after a while and his tears made patches on his face.

"Let me go, sister," he sniffed, "I must go—I must—I only wanted to know if you will come with me." Then when I demanded where he was going, he answered:

"To people who will feed, clothe and shelter us and ask nothing in return from us except that we worship their gods with them." And I knew who he spoke of, and I shrank at the thought.

"The Christians?" I spoke under my breath. "Do you mean the Christians?" He nodded defiantly, and then looked away.

"Oh Sidda," I cried, "Will you cut the bonds of relationship to forsake father, mother, brothers, sisters, neighbours and gods, all for handful of rice?" Sidda nodded. "I am hungry..." he said. "I am always hungry." And there was no answer to that.

Sidda joined the Christians who went about among the untouchables offering food and clothing, shelter and even learning for nothing more than the promise that we worship their god; who nursed the sick in the hospitals, brought medicines free to those who would not or could not go to them; who feared no defilement of touch....

"Why do you do it?" people asked them. "What do you get?" And they answered that their reward lay in another world, beyond this one. We were afraid of them, for they abused Mariamma and our gods, and tried to prevent us from sacrificing our cocks of worship and called these rituals evil and sinful practices and insisted that theirs was the only true god and the path they showed the only true path. If we gave up Mariamma and joined them they fed us and clothed us. If we gave up Mariamma—Mariamma from out of whose womb we had sprung, Mariamma who breathed in every drop of our blood and through every pore of our flesh! How could we give her up? But there were some who did.

Sidda said: "I will become a Christian, and when their water is sprinkled on me, then I will cease to be untouchable."

"If you think that, then you are a fool," I answered angrily. "You do not understand that we are born to our destiny because of actions in our past lives. What we have cooked we shall eat; what we have sown we shall reap. How can any magic water change your destiny?"

My mind faltered and I was not so sure, but I steeled myself and went on: "Whatever we do, in this life we will remain untouchable, for the gods have made us so. It is all a matter of the karma of our past lives."

Sidda said: "When I become a Christian I shall have food to eat and clothes to wear. And I shall go to school and learn to read and write."

"Sidda, Sidda," I cried in agony, "don't do this. Don't go from us. You must not try to change destiny. Who knows how Mariamma will punish you!"

But Sidda wrenched himself away from my grasp and ran from me.

The missionary people came for him one day to our untouchable quarters. They were a red-faced man and his wife. My father talked to them. "By your mercy," my father said, "he is a good boy and will serve you well." He stood humbly before them, hands joined.

"Not us, not us," they murmured, raising their eyes skywards, shaking their heads, and speaking in soft, gentle voices, "His will be the joy and the pride to serve the one and the true God, who is Jesus and who has had mercy upon this soul, and drawn it to him from its wanderings. From the weight of his sins shall this lamb be delivered today, by the mercy of our Lord in Heaven." They spoke earnestly but their words were beyond our understanding. Sidda looked down at the ground and his toes wiggled in the dust.

"Come child," said the missionaries. "We must go: the public baptisms are to be at sundown, and there are more who wish to come with us, and we must join them." At that I began to cry out: "Oh my brother, my brother," I sobbed. "Oh my brother, my brother.... Will you go from us, then?"

"Why do you weep, child?" said the missionary woman. "Do you not see that your brother will be fed and clothed? He will go to school, and you may visit him on a Saturday or a Sunday... and maybe, when you have seen the school, and when the Grace of God is upon you, maybe you too, child...."

But I turned and ran weeping. When my father came back he said to my mother and me: "Fools, why do you cry? Do you not understand that there they will feed and clothe him, and for us it will be one mouth less to feed? What does it matter? Is it too big a price to pay for a full belly?" He did not tell us that the missionary men had given him ten rupees for the boy, nor that for many days he could with the money buy his drink like a king, and not care.

Ponchu was angry when she heard about Sidda: "Could you not hold the boy back?" she raved, hobbling up and down the street. "Caste, khah... caste. What caste will these men give? You have sold the boy, and that is all there is to it." She spat derisively. Everyone could hear her. But there was no answer from my father. She went on abusing him: "And now with the money that you got from selling the boy, go, go... son of a pig, go and buy your drink, and then kill your wife with your beating." And so shouting over her shoulder for all the neighbourhood to hear, she hobbled into our hut.

"So they have taken the boy, have they, the missionary folk. What caste will they give, they who themselves are casteless? And you woman, you stood by and watched him go."

"What could I do, my sister?" my mother wept.

"The missionary men will feed him.... Is it too big a price to pay for a full belly? Tell me that."

But Ponchu who was not listening, hobbled out again upon her stick. "No, no," she said. "They shall not take him without a fight; that they shall not. Not when I live!" But Sidda went from us at the call of the Christian missionaries, and for all Ponchu's ranting and raving we could not hold him back.

So my two brothers nearest to me in age were gone and I felt lonely and sad. My mind continued to ask questions. Doubts raised their heads one after another and no one was able to solve them for me. My mother looked at me with frightened eyes when I asked her and cried out:

"Child, you must not say or think these things. You commit sin. You will be punished." And when I turned to Kantanna, he said: "I do not know, child. I have questions also in my mind, and doubts. The times we live in now are different. Mahatma Gandhi and his men travel over the country saying strange things. They say he is a Mahatma, and a man of God, but my mind is puzzled." He shook his head, in bewilderment locked and unlocked his fingers helplessly.

My questions remained unanswered, but they would not be silenced.

I thought often of the Christian missionaries after Sidda left us. I remembered snatches of what they said whenever they met us. The only people who did not shrink from us in disgust were the Christians. They said that in the eyes of the Christian god all men were equal. "I shall go to see Sidda," I told my mother some time after he had gone. "I shall see how he lives and we will know if he is happy and fed." My mother's eyes brightened, for we had not set eyes on Sidda since he had gone from us. Sometimes when we met the missionary people we asked them about him.

"Sidda?" they would answer smiling. "You would not know him if you saw him. Already he is in the second class at school. He is a clever boy. Come and see where he lives. You will never know until you have seen with your own eyes."

One Sunday I went to the Mission house, taking my courage in my hands. There was a sharp eyed girl at the Missionary house door. She eyed me with suspicion when I saw her. I tried instinctively to back away for fear of polluting her. She asked me what I wanted and I answered in a steady voice. "I have come for Sidda."

"What is your business with this boy?" she demanded sharply, possessively.

"He is my brother," I whispered. Her features grew gentler.

"Wait here," she told me. "The boys are at their singing. They will be out in a few minutes."

So I backed away and stood at a distance. After a while I began to hear the voices of children singing: I strained to listen and when the girl saw this she asked in a kinder voice: "Would you like to come and see?" and when I stammered "No—n—no," she continued, "All are welcome here. Do not think that untouchables are kept out.... This is a good place, and the people who look after you here are good and kind." Unable to contain myself any more I burst out:

"Tell me, mother, is my brother Sidda well?"

"Oh yes," answered the girl. Surprised at my doubt she continued in a smooth voice. "Why should he not be? He is a Christian, and that alone must bring him much happiness! Your brother is fortunate, and has nothing to fear. For now he is one of the blessed flock."

She spoke in a sing-song way, but her eyes darted sharply hither and thither like a bird's, as she continued: "He is a new person entirely. He even has a new name: Joseph Siddeshwara is his new name now. They call him Joseph."

"Joseph Siddeshwara. Joseph Siddeshwara!" Sidda had a name! Over and over I turned the name in my mind, savouring it, feeling its grandness and its importance, and I knew that she was right: Sidda had changed. He had a name now, a proper name! Unlike the rest of us untouchables who may only be called by nicknames—Boda and Chokka, Kunta and Kuruda. To have a name is to have a self on one's own, to be somehow made complete and whole.

"It is a great thing for him," the girl spoke on, raising her eyes to the roof. "His soul has been cleansed and redeemed and the gates of heaven thrown open to him." I looked up too, but there was nothing there except the great rafters of the building.

The singing ended. The boys came out into the compound led by the missionary man and woman. The girl went across and spoke to them. The missionary couple looked at me and smiled and nodded. And they all came to me with Sidda among them. When I saw him standing among them I knew that it was true that he had shed his untouchability and been made whole. The yellow sores had gone from the corners of his mouth and his eyes were clean now. He wore shorts and a shirt and had brown canvas shoes. But his eyes were angry and they said: "Why have you come? I have shed you with my untouchable past." The missionary couple said with pride: "Does your brother not look well? Why do you not come to us too?"

Sidda's eyes began to gleam. "Yes," said Sidda's eyes. "Why do you not come? Here they feed us well. Here we do not work carrying filth. What more can you want than that?" Aloud he said: "Yes, if you come here you will know the joy of serving the one and only true God." The missionary couple nodded and smiled, first at him, then at me. Then they left us together and withdrew. Sidda continued, as if it was part of the lesson he had to complete: "Our caste is higher than the Brahmin caste. We are Christians, and there is no caste higher than that."

But I could not accept it like that. The words stuck in my throat and choked me. When I found my voice, I said, "How does one know which gods were true and which were false?" and continued, "Besides, Sidda, if we were given caste who would clean the filth that men make?" He became silent and sullen. Distance fell between us. We had moved into different worlds. The missionaries joined us again. The man, plump, red-faced, balding said: "He looks well, does he not?" and put his arm around Sidda. I knew then that my brother was untouchable no more.... Where had his untouchability gone?

"Would you like to see the school?" said the missionary woman, drawing near. "There are girls there like you who learn many things. Come with me. I will show you the school."

I drew back, but she understood and said: "Here we are all of the Christian faith and we do not consider any one untouchable. Come." I trembled. But "Come," they said again and again. "No one is untouchable in the sight of our God, Yesu." I pushed back my fear of the sin of pollution and went with them into the school of the missionaries. I had never seen a place like this before. We went from room to room, and everywhere the walls were white and there were 'chicks' on the windows to soften the hardness of the sunlight, there were desks with benches for Sidda to sit on, and pictures on the walls....

The man and woman talked eagerly, pointed out and explained things to me. They led me to where the girls worked, embroidering on fine white cloth. They took my hand and led me, but I was trembling all the while. We went through all the rooms where the children ate and where they rested, where they played and where they learned to read and write.

The missionary woman said: "Do you see, child, do you see? All these things you could learn to do here, if you joined us. You look so clever. Why do you not come too?"

The bell rang, and the woman said: "It is prayer time. Come, child, let us join the children at their prayer in the house of God." I drew back, but she held my hand fast.

"Why, what is the matter, child?" she asked.

"I am untouchable," I answered, but the man smiled. "No

Children of God

one is untouchable in the sight of our God. Did I not say so before? Here in his dwelling place all may enter." So I entered too, though my knees would scarcely bear my weight for their trembling. The woman's grip of my hand was hard, as if she was afraid that if she let go I might suddenly vanish.

The house of prayer was clean and cool. The morning light splashed on the floor in colours. The girls sat in rows on benches on the side with smoothly combed hair, and in white sarees. All of them were reading. The boys sat on the other side and I spotted my brother among them. But he gave no sign that he noticed me.

He sat very solemn and still, hands clasping the book of prayer and songs. I sat down beside the woman. The man entered. He was in black clothes, and he went up before everyone and spoke in a very loud voice. Then of a sudden, a strange music rolled out, from where I could not tell. It filled the room and swelled into such a mountain of sound that the very rafters above us and the walls around us seemed to tremble. I was very afraid, and would have liked to run away. I looked around me in fear, but the others sat quietly, some with eyes closed, others turning over the pages of the book. The woman smiled at me in her motherly way, and I grew calmer. Then they all (and I with them) rose to their feet. They sang with much gesticulation. After this the man spoke to the assembled people. As he spoke he threw his hands up in the air, clenching his fist, and struck his chest. Scraps of his words and disjointed sentences struck my ears: "If you ask it will be given to you. If you knock on the door, it will be opened to you...."

"What? What will be given to them?" I thought.

"Listen to the story of Mary the Magdalene...." said the man. He told a story. As I listened I found I could understand. It was a story like the stories Kantanna tells, the story of a beautiful woman who lived in a city and sold herself to men for a living. She had long hair, which was her pride. All men admired her for her hair. She came one day to the house of a rich and learned man. That day he had invited Yesu to eat with him. She had heard of Yesu, and she was full of love and devotion for him, because he was a man of God. She ran in through the rooms of the house, past the rich and learned and great people, her hair flying behind her, and when she saw Yesu, she fell at his feet, weeping with love. Her tears washed his feet, and she wiped them with her hair. And then from the folds of her clothes she drew a box which contained a very precious and rare perfume. She poured this over his feet. Its fragrance filled the room. Now when the learned man and his friends saw this they were displeased.

"Can this man Yesu not tell who is clean and who unclean?" they murmured to each other. "How is it that he allows a woman like Mary to touch him?" But Yesu said to his host: "Why do you think these unkind thoughts, my friend? You are a priest. You should know better. Can you not see that this woman loves me more than anyone here does? I came to you—but you gave me no water to wash my feet. But this woman washed them with her tears, and wiped them with her hair, because of her great love. In your pride you forgot even to welcome me, but this woman has kissed my feet. You did not offer me oil for my head, but Mary has poured out a whole box of perfume on my feet. Can you not see how great her love is?"

The missionary man's voice grew very loud as he continued, but my mind wandered away. My thoughts began to wheel around again. A hundred questions, a hundred doubts flew in and out of my mind. When we came out of the temple the man and the woman said, both speaking together: "You must come again, child. Remember,—here all are received and all are welcome." Sidda had come and he stood between them, his eyes saying plainly: "It is good here. We do not work in filth. We are fed and our bellies are full. Why do you not come?"

As I went back homewards my mind was full of the story that the missionary man had told. But still I would not go Sidda's way...

The funeral is over. Kittu's outraged raw body has been covered with the wet, sweet-smelling mud, and he is lying beneath the earth. Kittu, my Kittu is dead and will never speak or laugh or weep again. The funeral drums are silent now. The people move homewards, and already Kittu has become a thing of the past, a memory. I hear the people talking, their voices are lighter now and their talk is about the present and the present problems, about feeding, and the price of rice and grain, about the sickness in one family and the celebration of a festival in another.

Mada says to me—"Come, let us go. It is over now. Why linger here? What good will that do?"

His face is naked in its misery, but he lifts me up and holds me so that I should not totter and fall. So leaning on him, I return home to our hut in the untouchable quarter, leaving Kittu there under the wet earth.

People continue to come to weep with us for Kittu, and to sing the songs of mourning. They are one with us in our sorrow. Mada says "Do you remember Father Pierre?" It is strange that Mada should think about Father Pierre, because I am thinking of him too, and at the mention of his name my eyes suddenly begin to brim over: my tears flow unchecked down my face. How can I forget Father Pierre?

"A missionary man," they called him but very soon we knew that though he too was born a Christian and worshipped the God of the Christians, he was still different from other men.

He came among the scavenger folk one day when Ponchu's granddaughter Sai was delivering her child. Ponchu was old and experienced in the delivering of children. She had delivered nearly every baby that had been born in the neighbourhood for many, many years. But when it was time for Sai's baby to come, and the pains had started, Ponchu found that the baby would not push its way through. A day and a night passed and though the girl was blue with screaming, the baby would not be born. All the women were with her now. "It will come," Ponchu cried. "It will come. A short while more, and the baby will be here, you will see...." But hour followed tortured hour, and the baby did not come.

I heard Ponchu swear angrily. Then she came to the door and faced us where we stood. "What are you waiting here for? Is this a temple fair that you crowd round to watch?" She brandished a great stick at us and the children scattered away and fled—all except I. I did not fear Ponchu, and she did not threaten me. So I remained where I was.

After a while Linga's wife came out. "Old Aunt," she cried to Ponchu, "The girl is sweating all over.... The body is cold.... Perhaps if the missionary doctor came!" But Ponchu was adamant. "I will see," she muttered. "I will see how this baby thwarts me! No, there shall be neither mission nor pission doctor. What do you take me for?" But as the day advanced, the baby was no nearer birth than it had been. I waited, because Sai was my friend. After a while suddenly there was no sound at all—not even Ponchu's voice. Linga's wife came out again, her face ghost-white and her eyes stricken.

"Is the baby come, my mother?" I asked.

She whispered: "Child, run to the Mission Hospital in Manur. A doctor *must* come—we cannot wait any more—."

"Is the baby come, my mother?" I asked again, helplessly and stupidly.

But she pushed me: "Oh don't stop to talk, child. Go on, run. If you do not run and get a doctor then Sai might die. Go, please go... there is a foreign doctor in the hospital. He might prick her with the needle and bring her to life. Go, go, take the bus to Manur and before evening you will be there. Here take this for your bus ticket, if you sit at the back, perhaps upon the floor, then nobody will mind...." She gave me a silver eight anna bit, and I ran, never stopping till I came to the Venugopalapuram bus-stand.

How clear that journey is in my mind today. I can remember still, standing at the bus-stop, a little way away because there were many people waiting to travel in the bus. A fat priest with the caste marks on his forehead, some Gandhi men, who in those days were everywhere, dressed in homespun cloth, and white caps on their heads. I was afraid that the priest would see me and recognise me for a scavenger. I stood apart from the others. The conductor bade everyone get in, and they climbed into the bus at his word. But now that the time had come I was afraid, because though I had known some scavengers of my caste who had gone in a bus, I had never been in one myself. I stood outside, and the conductor said:

"Go in, get in, slut, we cannot wait for you all day long. Do you want music and drumming before you step in?" Then I climbed in. The conductor pointed to a seat. But I hesitated, and the priest turned and growled.

"An untouchable!", he pointed out to the conductor. "She is a scavenger. How can she sit in the bus?"

"Times have changed," the conductor laughed cheekily. "There is pollution in the air we breathe, Brahman priest, and little to be done about it except to go home and cleanse yourself. In the bus all may sit if the money they pay is good money." And he twirled a coin in the air to test it. He turned to me and said carelessly:

"Go, go and sit over there in the corner."

Trembling in every nerve, I took the seat he had pointed out. I was saying, again and again, the name of Mariamma, to give myself strength, and I sat on the seat's extreme edge. We waited for a while longer. Just as the bus began to start on its way, there was a shout outside, and a man came running, "Wait... we are coming... wait a while..." So the bus waited. The man shouted to his family to hurry up, that the bus would not wait for them for ever. He climbed into his seat and shouted to his family to hurry, and after a while they all came in, his wife and his mother and several children, and a servant-boy under a big green trunk. They all sat down in different seats. The wife and mother came to the seat where I was sitting already, and they were about to sit when the wife saw me and instantly knew me: "It is the scavenger girl," she shrieked, "Ayya, it is a scavenger..." More people entered the bus. It was full now. "Sit now, sit, sit, what do you stand there for?" her husband shouted, "Why do you not sit? You will lose your place."

" There is a scavenger sitting upon this seat," the woman shrieked back. "How can I sit?"

The man did not take notice of what she said. He cursed and ordered her to sit down at once. And the conductor laughed cheekily all the while. The woman took her seat but she kept getting up every few seconds and would not be quiet even when the bus started to go. "How can I sit, I ask you; there is a scavenger girl sitting here: Can you not see? It is all very well for you to shout from there."

Then the old woman took up and began to grumble aloud.

"That is why I swore I would stay behind at home. But you had to drag me as well and have me polluted, and make me sit with scavengers and tanners and all kinds of untouchables: I am an old woman, in the evening of my life. Was it necessary that I be subjected to this—pollution from a scavenger? Was it necessary?"

I did not know what to do. The bus was moving fast; besides, I had paid the money and bought my ticket, so I knew I had a right to go. And besides too if I did not go and fetch the doctor then perhaps Sai would die. That was the thought that hammered in my head. If I did not go, Sai might die.

So I sat there, saying nothing, full of fear and anxiety, full of prayers to Mariamma. I did not look at them either, but fixed my eyes on my feet, and my ears were hot with the sound of their angry words:

"Ayya, ayya, she sits there, as if she were a queen," the woman said. "Don't I know her.... Her mother scavenges in the house of Venkatamma my cousin.... carries the filth and the daughter rides the bus with people of caste!..."

"Stop the bus, stop the bus," wailed the old woman, "I tell you, I will go no further! It is an outrage! Either the scavenger will get off the bus, or...."

"Mother do not make so much noise, sit down," shouted the conductor.

"Yes, sit down," she echoed glaring at him, "Sit down with the scavenger girl on my lap... that is what you would like, would you not?"

The boy, shrugging his shoulders, said: "Anyone who has bought a ticket with money may travel in the bus. Those are the rules of the Company."

"The Company or the company's father!" cried the old woman. "What is that to me? I will not have myself polluted in this old age. My son has paid too, let me remind you."

"Fools, what a noise you are making," said the man to his womenfolk. "Sit down, I say. . . ." His voice was so angry that his wife sat down on the same seat where I sat, edging away from me as far as she could go, and then the other found a seat further away, and there was some peace after that. I could feel the woman beside me tense with anger, glowering at me from time to time. The priest took up where the two women had left.

"There are no morals left anywhere in the world," he grumbled. "What are we coming to, now with all the scavengers and washermen and grasscutters and cobblers sitting alongside of priests and men of caste. The arrogance of these people is becoming insufferable."

The Gandhi men answered: "Times are changing, ayya. How can you stop the passage of time and the changes that will come."

The woman spluttered angrily: "Keep your words, young man. Do you presume to teach your betters? Perhaps you are a Gandhi man, yes, it is this Gandhi disease that has caught and spread, that makes these scavengers so arrogant." But before the young man could answer that, one of the other passengers opened the newspaper and began to read out aloud.

"It says here that Mahatma Gandhi has gone to Delhi to speak with the Viceroy, Irwin. No doubt he will ultimately bring us our freedom. It looks hopeful."

The priest said: "The Gandhi men talk of opening

temples and schools to the untouchables. Who will eat the fruit of this sin if these things should happen?"

"The untouchables are Harijans." One of the Gandhi men answered, "Children of God. It is no sin to accept them as brothers."

The priest shook his head and fell silent, but his eyes were angry and disapproving. The man with the family turned round. He had diamond rings on his fingers and diamonds hung in his ears. "I can read," he said, "I am educated. I am a contractor; I take toddy shop contracts." Everyone stared at him, respect mingled with interest and curiosity. The diamonds flashing in his ring were a sign of wealth and ever increasing prosperity. "I read the newspapers, too," continued the man and they shook their heads admiringly. "Gandhiji may be a man of God, but I fear much of his talk will bring about trouble in the land. This talk of untouchables being equal to men of caste—it will bring nothing but trouble."

"Gandhiji is a man of God," said the young man earnestly, "he brings the message of freedom to the people."

"How can one be free from one's destiny?" countered the priest, cunningly. "It is not good to go against the laws of the gods," and the toddy shop contractor echoed, waving his hand: "It is not good, no, it is not good. If we do not have a care, these people will become our equals and we will have no position left." After this everyone fell silent as the bus went on. They began to nod and go to sleep, their heads rolling from side to side. Only the woman who was next to me continued to be taut and angry. I thought helplessly and miserably: "What can I do? I must get a doctor or Sai might die." I hoped in my heart that heaven would forgive me if I had sinned.

After a while we reached Manur, and the woman quickly moved away to a place that fell vacant and I, thankful that no worse had happened that day, quickly left the bus. I knew of the time when Bikka, one of my cousins had gone by bus and he had been thrown out, then mobbed and beaten. He had come home with a broken nose and mud in his hair and eyes and on his body. I had known of others too. But today the goddess had been merciful to me, and I came to the Manur Mission Hospital with its red tiled roof and its white walls. It was there at the mission hospital that I met Father Pierre.

The place was crowded with the sick and the diseased who came to be treated. Diseased women, diseased children, children with sores and children with burns, children with fevers, with swollen bellies and withered faces; they groaned and cried and called out for help. Father Pierre sat on a bench in a corner waiting, with a child in his arms. He had taken her to relieve the mother, who was weak with a fever and tuberculosis. One of the mission foreign ladies came up to him and stood talking to him. A young girl, much like the one that I had seen in Sidda's school, stood at the door.

"Please, my mother," I burst out going to her, "Please, my mother, they have sent me for a doctor for Sai. Her baby will not be born, and now she might die."

"Where is the patient?" the girl asked.

"At home—beyond Venugopalapuram, I rode in the bus to come here...."

"Beyond Venugopalapuram? Where?" questioned the girl, and I told her, "The untouchables' quarter."

"Wait here," said the girl, "I will see what the doctor says."

She disappeared behind a door, and I stood against a pillar waiting. It was then that I became conscious of Father Pierre's presence. He was a tall man, tall like a tree, thin like a reed, and slightly stooping. His face was wrinkled and lined, a thin face with the bones showing and blue eyes that twinkled like small flames. He was wiping his spectacles. The missionary woman had gone away. Presently Father Pierre saw me and moved up a little on the bench to make place for me. He motioned me to sit down, But I drew back, because willingly and needlessly I would not defile, and the memory of the happenings in the bus was raw in my mind. Just then the girl came back. "The doctor is too busy," she told me. "Can your relative not be brought to the hospital?" My heart sank at the thought of returning empty-handed to the waiting people.

"Then it will not be till tomorrow, before the doctor sees Sai," I cried out in despair.... "And already, already the hand of death is on her."

The girl shrugged her shoulders.

"Perhaps," she agreed with a worldly-wise look in her eyes. "But what is one to do?" She turned to the man and said to him: "This is the trouble with these people. They do not come till it is too late. Why could she not have come earlier?" I opened my mouth to speak, but the girl went on still speaking to Father Pierre: "I have been asked to tell you, sir, that they do not need your services here. The doctor says you may go. This is a Methodist hospital."

"I cannot go home empty-handed, my mother," I cried out.

"The doctor is a human being like you and me," said the girl to that. "He has only two hands and he can only be in one place at a time. He is very busy now. Later, perhaps."

"But later Sai will die... and her baby—" I was weeping. "I

fall at your feet, my mother, I beg on my knees—".

The girl shrugged her shoulders. "What can I do?" she said. I turned slowly to go down the steps. It was then that the Father Pierre spoke to me. "I am a doctor," he said, putting a hand lightly on my shoulder. "I will come with you."

That was how Father Piere came into my life and into the lives of the untouchables of Venugopalapuram. We walked down to the gate together and at the gate he said: "I have a bicycle. It will be easier to ride on it than to walk. You can climb at the back and hold my box of medicines, and so we will get to the bus stop. After that they will shove the cycle on the top and the bus will carry it for me."

"Master," I said, uttering the words fearfully, "I am an untouchable. I am of the scavenger's caste. I will walk, my master."

But Father Pierre did not seem to understand. First he looked at me with a puzzled look, and then he smiled: "An untouchable, eh? Of the sweeper caste? Well, no matter. I am one myself! Besides we must not delay, because your friend is very ill, and a bicycle will get us there sooner." So without further protest. I climbed upon the back of his bicycle and held his bag of medicines with one hand, and with the other clutched at the seat to keep myself from falling off, and I told him which way to go. So he pedalled with all his strength till we reached the bus stop, and finally arrived home in the untouchable quarter of Venugopalapuram where the scavengers lived.

Father Pierre saved Sai's life. Sai herself lay still and ashen, so that they feared for a while that it was all over with her too, and Ponchu beat her forehead and wept. But Sai lived. Father Pierre came out of their hut in the early hours of the morning, wiping his spectacles; the women of the quarters had already gathered outside Ponchu's hut to sing the songs of mourning. "The girl will live," said Father Pierre. "If you look after her well, she will recover her strength."

We stared at him unbelieving. He had wrested her from the hands of Yama. I remember how the daylight rippled before my eyes, because I was weeping with joy and seeing all things through my tears. The people gathered around Ponchu's mud hut, and they were weeping too. Soma was biting her lip and making grunting noises. After a while each one who sat there silently made a separate vow to Mariamma, to offer her this and that—some said an anna's worth of oil for her lamp, and others coconuts and plantains, others grain or sugar, flowers and incense, all if Sai should be restored. But Ponchu promised a goat in sacrifice if the girl should recover.

When Father Pierre came out among us, we all moved away to the mango tree which was the meeting place of the scavenger people. Someone gave him water from a kerosene tin to wash his hands and his face, and when he was clean, he joined us there. Then the women sang songs of gratitude and praise to him, calling him their hero, their god, their father and mother and the light of their eyes. They danced around him clapping their hands, and when that was done, we stood waiting for him to speak. But what he said surprised and baffled us: "I have no home to go to," he told us. "I am a stranger here in Venugopalapuram. I was travelling down from Bhadrapura. I had left my bed and bundle on my bicycle while I went to attend to a sick man. When I came out my bundle was gone. And I have nothing, save the clothes I wear and my box of medicines. Can one of you give me a bed to sleep on for tonight?" He said this very simply and quietly, as if it were the most natural thing in the world for a man to seek shelter for the night in the untouchable people's quarter.

And because it was so simply said, we looked at each other puzzled, and for some time nobody answered. He tried again as if striving to make things easier: "I do not need anything very much, my friends, only somewhere to sleep: I am a wanderer."

Still we said nothing in answer, for we did not know at all what to make of this strange man, and this unforeseen situation. Father Pierre looked from face to face. He was taller than any of the men there, but in spite of his height, he looked alone and helpless as a child. He looked at each one of us and then at last he said: "If it is not possible for me to stay here then perhaps I could find some other place. But could you tell me any that you know. I am a stranger here in Venugopalapuram."

At this point Soma came forward and spoke: "Swami, stay with us. We can find a place for you." Her voice was very gentle. When she said this many voices spoke:

"It is true, master," they said, echoing her. "What the girl says is true. It is not as though we did not want you: forgive us for not showing more welcome. But we were afraid, for we are scavenger folk—and we are of the untouchable caste. But if the master will stay with us, then master, it will be as if the Deity from the temple had himself walked down and come in our midst."

Father Pierre said, "I am grateful to you, my friends, I have nowhere to go, and would like to rest before I continue on my wanderings."

The men began to run in different directions, and to confer among themselves and with Soma as to how they should make him comfortable. Kantanna and his family offered to sleep in Linga's place that night and give him the use of their hut, because it was the biggest, and cleanest. It has a little mud courtyard that Kantanna's wife washed out everyday with cow-dung. And Yanka said he had an old mattress that he could offer if the Swami would accept it, and Thimma had a goat's hair blanket, the coarse and rough kind village folk use ; it was very old and thread-bare, but it was all he had and he would offer it gladly. Kantanna had a wooden bed in his courtyard, and my mother declared she would give an old mat which we had in the house.

But after a while Father Pierre asked humbly, as if afraid that he was making a nuisance of himself, "I am thirsty. Could I have some water to drink?"

And again we all looked at each other not knowing what to answer, but this time we did what he asked without argument. I ran into our hut and brought the tin in which we stored the water and as I poured it out my heart was very full and reverent.

The people stood a little way away watching him. He drank thirstily and long, and when he had finished he looked up, his beard still wet, and he smiled warmly and gratefully.

In my heart for a while I had wondered if I had sinned. For water touched by an untouchable is polluted and the sin of an untouchable who pollutes (so I had been told) is many hundred times greater than the sin of the man who is polluted. But I could not help asking myself, "Is it a sin to give a thirsting man water?"

I took my courage into my hands. "Swami," I said, "you have not eaten. Are you not hungry, my master?"

He smiled: "I...I am, child," he confessed hesitantly, "my last meal was in the morning yesterday before I left Bhadrapura."

I ventured on: "Master, may I bring you food to eat?"

My people stared at me unbelieving but no one spoke.

"I am grateful, child," said Father Pierre, "but already you have given me more than it is right for me to ask."

At that they all protested in one voice. "No, no, master; don't say so, master. Let us bring you food, we are poor folk, but let us bring food."

So he ate what we gave him—rice and sauce and some spinach that Kantanna's wife quickly cooked and jaggery crushed into freshly grated coconut to sweeten the mouth, for it was as if the Deity himself from the temple had come among us, and even in the midst of our poverty we must give him of our best.

"You are too kind to me," he protested, and we remonstrated with him: "Master, do not say that. It is you, who have been kind to us." And because such a thing had never happened to us before in our lives, we had no words to say all that we felt.

Father Pierre slept in the hut that night. The next morning he spoke to the men of the community.

"Which is the road to Nagavelur? There is a small hospital there where I heard they need a doctor . . . so I was told. Perhaps I could go there and work."

The men did not answer at once. One thought was in their minds but they could not speak it easily. They stood around him undecided until Soma prompted Kantanna:

"Well, why don't you speak, Grandfather? Go on and say what is in your mind."

Kantanna voiced everyone's thoughts: "Master," he said, "stay with us. We are poor folk, but all we have is yours, master. Why must you go further? To us you are the Deity himself come from the temple."

Father Pierre laughed a little, shaking his head: "I am no

Deity from the temple, my friends, only a simple old man; a homeless wanderer. People tell me I am mad, and it may be that I am, in their lights. They are angry with me too because my thoughts and theirs don't seem to agree. So I have had to wander by myself seeking out my own path, thinking my own thoughts. If I could make myself a hut and live here with you, my friends, I would be grateful and happy."

Kantanna said, "Stay with us, master, though we have nothing to offer you except poverty."

From that day on Father Pierre made his home with our people and began to live in the Venugopalapuram scavenger quarters. Later when we talked of these happenings among ourselves, Kantanna said to us all:

"Why are you surprised? Have you not heard stories of how the temple Deity has gone out and lived among untouchables and even done their scavenging for them? Why should we wonder at him? Perhaps he is God himself come to us."

"Perhaps!" agreed the people, and then again and again, wagging their heads wisely repeated: "It cannot be otherwise. He must be the Deity from the temple."

We asked no more questions for we had found an answer to this man. He was the Deity, and the miracle of Sai confirmed our belief. There was an old hut that no one occupied. The roof had fallen in. Only the mud walls stood. "It is a good enough place for me." Father Pierre said, and we hung our heads, ashamed that in our poverty it was all the shelter that we could offer him.

He worked with the men as they made the roof for him with plaited palm leaf; the women smeared fresh cow-dung on the walls and the floor. Soma suggested that we draw patterns with white powder on the floor all around the hut, and string mango leaves over the entrance, to show our gratitude for Sai's recovery. Kantanna brought the wooden bed in and put it in the room, and the place was ready. When Father Pierre saw how the hut had been transformed he laughed happily and his blue eyes lit up with child-like pleasure. That was how he came into our lives, and as the days went by we forgot to wonder at him and ceased to think that he was different from us. As he had accepted us so we too accepted him. Only we never forgot in our hearts that he was the Deity in the guise of Father Pierre. For God we knew, because he was God, cannot be polluted as men can.

Father Pierre lived among us as if he were one of us. When we were sick he treated us with medicines. In his old leather bag he carried his mixtures, and ointments, pills, and needles. We took to him children who were ill, who had sores or festering wounds, or the Eyes, or the Shivering fever, and he gave them medicines.

I took my baby sister to him. All over her little body she had thick clusters of yellow sores, from which the pus oozed. He held her to him and asked, "How long has she had these sores?"

"For three months, my master," I answered him. "She began to have them soon after she was born." I explained how my mother had plastered them over with cow-dung and ash which are said to heal sores. I told him how Mariamma's priest had broken three coconuts for her because a devil troubled her, and had to be appeased with food.

All the while that I spoke, Father Pierre had been cleaning the sores with cotton wool and medicine water. He murmured from time to time little endearments to the baby in his arms. He did not answer me. When he had cleaned the sores, he smeared some yellow ointment on them. Then handing the tube to me he said: "Take this, child; apply it again tonight. It will be better than cow-dung. Cow-dung is not safe to apply on sores."

I plucked up courage: "You are so kind and so good, Swami," I said. "Why do you do this for us, poor scavenger folk who are untouchable?"

"I do this because I hope that in this way I may find God!"

"Who is this god, Swami, that you are looking for?" I persisted. "I do not know," he answered vaguely, frowning a little and shaking his head: "because I have not found him."

I can see again the face of the bearded priest who came into our lives. He sat with us and shared our rice. He shared our lives and was one of us. Where is he now? We ask vainly, because no one knows and no one answers. They charged him with preaching a foreign religion, with converting the people to a foreign faith. Strangers we had never seen before in our quarters came shouting: "Father Pierre, go back, go back."

Father Pierre came out at the sound of their voices. "Go back where? This is my home, these are my people. Where shall I go?" said Father Pierre, whom we called Swami.

"Foreign Priest," they yelled, "we want no foreign missionaries in our midst."

"The Swami is one of us!" said Kantanna loudly. "His home has been with us for many years. It is you who are strangers. We have never seen you before."

That made them uneasy. They stood apart, their eyes angry and threatening, and then after a while they went. But when they were at some distance they began to shout again: "Go back. Foreigner go back! False Priest go back." But all this came many years later. At the time that I speak of

Father Pierre lived with us and was one of us. We did not remember at all that the colour of his skin was different or that he was a foreigner.

We spoke to him and laughed with him. Sometimes we sat without speaking; we sat in silence, thinking our vague, misty thoughts. He was always there when we needed him. His medicines cured our ailments. But sometimes death came, and then he stayed with the family, and his presence brought them comfort. If people, who brought him their sick, said to him: "Swami, perhaps we should sacrifice a fowl to Mariamma," he shook his head and, frowning a little, answered gently, "A fowl does not come for nothing, my friends. It costs money that you have earned with hard work, and which would buy food for your children. And would God want from you the blood of a little chicken in payment for making your sick one well? Would he wish to snatch from you what you earn and what would feed your little ones, would he?"

But if the sick men grew uneasy and feared Mariamma's anger, then Father Pierre would say: "Very well, if the offering of a fowl will make your heart lighter, then offer it. But also eat the medicine that I give you. Either the fowl or my medicine will make you well, and if you are well, then, that is what really matters, is it not? What does it matter what it was that cured you?" and his eyes would crease into a smile. Every morning he climbed upon his bicycle and went down the road to visit other villages and treat the sick who could not get to the hospital, just as he had treated Sai in our quarters.

One day he asked me if I could help him with his work. "It is not easy for me to do it alone," he said.

"Swami!" I cried, "but I am ignorant and unlearned!"

He smiled, and went on: "You can learn, child. You are a quick and clever girl."

"What can I learn, Swami? I am untouchable." But there was excitement stirring inside me. I longed for him to say more and he did. He would not give in. Before long he had overcome my reluctance and my hesitation and persuaded me to come and learn to read and write. And as the days passed others began to come with me: first the children came, and following them came the parents, giggling and shy, timid, excited, curious and full of eagerness. Only Soma would not come. She stood outside her hut as we went past and looked at us with scorn and mockery in her eyes.

"Why don't you come with us, Soma?" I called and she threw back her head. "Will reading and writing fill the belly?" she cried. "Tell me that!"

"A man is not belly alone!" I retorted, and my companions smiled and applauded my answer.

Soma was not to be silenced.

"When a man is hungry," she answered, her eyes flashing "then he is little more than belly. Your books will not cool his hunger."

One day Soma grabbed me by the shoulder roughly; "Look, girl," she began. "For our people to learn to read and write will not be good."

"Why, what are you saying?" I cried, but Soma silenced me with an impatient wave of her hand. "Look, girl—now our people are contented. They do not question. They have Mariamma's shrine and the festivals in the shrine, and the feeding in the temple to keep them contented. If they learn to read and write, their minds will stir. They will begin to have thoughts. Thoughts will become questions and murmurs. They will begin to want to know why they are untouchable. They will begin to look upon themselves as human and after that they will demand human treatment." She paused for a second and probed my eyes with her own as if she dared me to face the situation. Then she questioned harshly: "And where will this lead to? Tell me, where will this lead to?"

"I—I—don't know," I whispered. "I don't understand.

"Oh, you are a fool. Can you not see, stupid one, that all these things will lead to trouble?"

I shook my head in bewilderment. It had always seemed to me that it was good to learn to read and write. But suddenly Soma had shown another side to it and made me afraid and unsure.

Old Ponchu was another grumbler:

"Why, what do the scavenger folk want with reading and writing?" she complained. "What is the world coming to?" But she laughed as she said it and secretly encouraged Sai to join the others.

But the excitement of learning did not last. After a while one by one the people dropped out. Only I stayed on with Sai and Mada. My hands grew wet with the strain of forming the letters; my head reeled with trying to remember them. At home I would turn over in my mind again and again, the things that he had taught and, after a while, slowly, like light piercing through the palls of heavy darkness, understanding would come to me. And so I began to read. I stumbled and faltered but, nevertheless, I could read. I could read! The rows of black letters in books, in scraps of newspaper that I found on the roadside, these had up to then been no more than unfathomable mysteries to me. But now printed sentences in my torn text unfolded wonderful secrets, wonderful because of their coherence and completeness.

"The rain falls upon the grass," I would read, slowly, fearfully, and then suddenly the meaning and significance of that simple sentence burst upon me like a great ray of light, and I would feel the raindrops and hear them and smell them in the dust. I knew then that Soma had been wrong in spite of all her worldly wisdom. After my work, I would sit down in some secret corner and follow with my eyes and fingers the magic words and sentences in the books that Father Pierre gave me. They came out of an old tin trunk that he had brought with him, the day when he came back from one of his visits to the city. It was full of old, worn books, with moth-eaten, crumbling pages that had grown yellow and musty with age. Father Pierre gave each to me saying: "I think you will like this book." The books revealed to me a new world I had not even dreamed of in my wildest fancies. They cast a spell over me, and changed me from within.

Those were happy days—the days when I worked with Father Pierre. He taught many things, the way to mend a tear in cloth and patch it; the way to make a poultice for an absess; the way to tie a bandage and bathe the fevered bodies of convulsive children. He taught me how to boil the needle he used and to read the fever stick, to treat the people who came with burns and bites and wounds. When we were not working he spoke to me of many things and I listened intently, for each word he said was precious to me. He told me of people who lived and worked beyond the confines of Venugopalapuram and beyond the shores of our land. He told me of his travels: he spoke of the blue sea and giant ships that sailed over it, of the cities of Europe and of America and the great rivers of the Chinese folk and the high velds of the Africans. His words were like the light of dawn flooding the darkness of my mind and waking it gently to life.

I did not notice how the days slipped away from my life and I was suddenly a child no more but a woman. One day my mother stared at me suddenly as if I was a stranger. And then after a while she sent for Ponchu who was her adviser on all matters. When Ponchu came the two spoke together and Ponchu said, reflectively, rolling betel leaves on her palm: "You are grown now, girl, and it is time to think of sending you to the house of your betrothed." At this I started and took a swift frightened breath. Ponchu laughed. "What are you afraid of, foolish child? Mada is a good man and does not drink. His father does not drink nor does he beat his wife. These are things that must be considered of a man. Your mother wishes that I speak to Mada's parents to fix the day for the wedding." She broke off and put yet another wad of betel into her mouth. Panic swept over me, and Ponchu seeing how my face changed chuckled, clapping her hands together:

"Ayya, Ayya," she laughed. "The girl is shy, what did I tell you? She longs to be a bride. It is a good sign for a girl to be shy." My face grew hot; and my eyes and neck burned.

"I have not many days to live, child," my mother took up now "and before I go, I must send you to your man."

Ponchu laughed and said, "Don't talk of dying, sister. You will live to see Nagi wedded, never fear. And you will live to see that worthless Boda married too."

I could not bear to hear any more. I turned from them and fled, my face and ears burning. I ran until I reached the shrine. The little wick lights inside it were glimmering and flaring, casting dancing shadows upon the walls. No one was there, not even Mariamma's priest. I sat on the stone step, and held my head in my hands, and I began to murmur the name of the Goddess in an effort to still the storm in my heart. The face of the man whose image was in my heart came back before me.

The man I worshipped, I had seen him in Father Pierre's hut. There were four people who had come to Father Pierre to speak to him, three men and a young woman, and among them was Acharya Harishchandra, the Teacher. On the day that I saw him for the first time I had combed out my hair and plaited it. The braid lay heavy and glossy in my hands. I was proud because nobody among my people had hair as black and as soft and as thick. I had worn a clean sari of a bright gay yellow which Father Pierre had given me, and its freshness and purity enclosed me. So dressed I went down to Father Pierre's hut. My mother sighed when she saw me so turned out, and Ponchu whom I crossed in the lane shouted after me:

"Have you taken leave of your senses completely, fool, that you dress like a woman of caste? A full sari for a scavenger! Why, what madness are you starting?"

Other people stared too as I went by, and a woman sitting by the wayside picking lice from a child's hair, said: "You do not realise, foolish girl, that you may be stoned and beaten for your pride."

I trembled inside me, knowing that what they said was true. An untouchable in a clean washed sari, her body covered completely—would they stone me for my transgression? Would they tear my limbs apart for this crime against the ancient law? And yet I went on in my full yellow sari which was so crisp and new and so beautiful. And I felt an elation even in spite of my fear. Why had I taken such care that day to appear beautiful? Had something, someone whispered to my heart that he would be there?

When I entered Father Pierre's hut, I saw him. There were three others beside him and they were sitting with Father Pierre, and seemed to be talking earnestly of important matters. Nor did the woman remain silent; she spoke like the rest of them and they paid careful attention to her words. She was a beautiful woman, I thought. She spoke freely to the men and when she spoke they leaned forward to listen: the language she used was refined, and sounded to me like music. All of them were Gandhi folk, judging by the clothes they wore. They sat on the floor together, cross-legged in the manner of people of refinement and caste, and when I came into the room they raised their heads and looked at me. Father Pierre smiled and welcomed me and told them my name. He held out his hand to me: "Come," he said, "Come and meet our friends." I found myself facing the Acharya then, and for a moment I stood there as if I had turned to rock. Then a confusion surged over me, a shyness so sudden and powerful and overwhelming that I turned and ran, never stopping till I reached my home.

"What is it, girl?" my mother asked. But I answered nothing. The next day when Father Pierre went by on his rounds, he called to me:

"Child, why did you run like that, what happened?"

I felt myself blush: "I...I do not know," I faltered. "I...I perhaps I was afraid."

"Why?" he asked, "What was there to fear?" I remained silent, my eyes upon the ground.

Father Pierre said gently: "What need is there for fear, child? They were the people from the city whom I had spoken to you about, do you remember? Acharya Harishchandra is a dear friend of mine, and the others are his co-workers." Then he told me that they were travelling around the country, to live in the villages. Acharya Harishchandra had offered to help him. He would live here and have a school where people would be taught to read and write and spin and weave. Maybe as time went on, to do other things...oil pressing, sugar-cane crushing and such like. "Will that not be a good thing?" asked Father Pierre.

"Yes, father," I nodded, "It will be a good thing." But the thoughts in my secret mind were saying all the while: "How like a shining god he is! How like a god to be worshipped!"

With my lips I said to Father Pierre: "Where will they live, Swami?" and he answered, "He will live here with me, but the others will make their home in Venugopalapuram where the school will be. At first only reading and writing will be taught with spinning and weaving."

"It is strange that they should leave the comfort of their lives and come to spend their time here—why, what would they gain?" I spoke hesitantly.

"More than you imagine, child," Father Pierre answered. "Their gains would not be counted in the ordinary currency of money—silver and copper coins."

"In what then?"

But he leaned forward and changing the topic asked: "Would you like to go to the Acharya's school?"

When I found my voice to answer him, I said: "How can I go to school in Venugopalapuram, my master? Do you forget that I am of the scavenger caste and untouchable?" But Father Pierre did not think this was reason enough.

"That is no matter," he said. "All are welcome in this school." I stared at him.

"But he is—he is a man of caste—an Acharya. How can it be?"

Father Pierre replied: "You have heard of Mahatma Gandhi, have you not? Acharya Harishchandra and his friends are followers of the Mahatma, entrusted to do this work by the Mahatma himself."

I understood now. For we too in our untouchables' quarters, poor and unlettered as we were, had heard of the Mahatma. Never had we set our eyes on him, but we knew that he was a man above men, a man of God.

I found myself thinking continually about the Acharya; my mind wandered often from me to dwell upon the memory of his beauty, the radiance of his eyes, the strength and the grace of his body. In the mornings when I worked cleaning the filth of Venugopalapuram, my mind held him, refusing to let him go. Wherever I went, he was with me, and I could not forget him. When our people spoke to me I did not hear, and often when they passed me by in the lane, I did not see or greet them.

"What is the matter with the girl?" Ponchu charged my mother loudly and within my hearing. "Believe me, my sister," she continued in her shrewd voice, "these are nothing but signs that the girl has ripened, and is ready for marriage. If you wait much longer, it will be too late, and her youth will have gone. Now is the time." But when my mother asked me again, I answered: "Wait awhile, please wait a while, do not send me from you."

And because I earned them their food my mother held her peace and my father growled out: "Let her be. You do not carry her weight on your head, do you? The rice that she eats she earns. So why do you not let her be? And if she goes, who is to mind the children?"

I saw the Acharya many times in Father Pierre's hut.

Some instinct, unerring and un-understandable, would quiver in the depths of my spirit and I would know even before I entered the hut that he would be there.

He did not speak to me. For many days it seemed to me that he did not even notice me. Father Pierre took him and his friends round the untouchable quarter. He pointed out to them the filth of Venugopalapuram where the naked children played in the dust; the hovels like sores upon the earth. The women came and watched them from afar, and when they approached drew back dreading that they might sin by brushing against them. Father Pierre took them with him to the back street behind the Venugopalapuram temple on the temple feast day, and they looked at food being thrown to the untouchable people. He took them too round the streets while the scavengers worked, and they crossed my path one day when I walked down with the bucket of filth upon my head. I cast my eyes down, ashamed to have them see me as a carrier of human filth. I walked on the edge of the street, fearful that I or my shadow might touch and pollute. And when Father Pierre worked in the untouchable quarter, treating the sick, the young Teacher and his friends watched him.

When they came back to Father Pierre's hut, from the round of the streets, the Teacher's face was ablaze with anger.

"Why must these things be?" he said in a loud and angry voice. Father Pierre did not look up. He was dressing the wounds of a child who had burnt herself badly. The mother had treated the burns with ashes from Mariamma's shrine. When Father Pierre cleaned the child's arm, the wounds gaped in large blotches of red and yellow. I handed him the bandages and the bottles.

The Teacher said: "There will be no progress until these

evils are set right." and his voice was still angry. Then he got up, and his head nearly touched the low roof. He began to pace the room.

"These things are a blot on our name, a disgrace to our nation and must be eradicated." My senses began to reel in my head as I heard him and set it throbbing. The Teacher continued to thunder:

"Do our scriptures themselves not speak of the equality of man in the sight of God?" He turned round and stood facing Radha who came with them, "Why, why, why, for all their wisdom; why will they not see light?" His voice was so angry and loud that the child looked at him and started to cry in fear, and had to be consoled. I thought in a daze:

"Even in his anger, how beautiful he is, how beautiful!" I continued to work, putting the things away. The Teacher went on, spreading his arms out: "Will these things go on for ever? Whatever is done, it is like a drop in the ocean, a speck in the sky, and you are where you were before." And he sat down and clenching his hands, rested his head on them as if he had suddenly wearied of everything.

Radha nodded: "That is how it seems," she remarked. "But there is no other solution. We are pledged to this—and now there is no turning back. Our boats are burnt."

Father Pierre spoke, as he wound the bandage around the child's arm: "These things are evil, and must be changed. And they can be changed if you have faith, because all things are possible if you have faith." But the young Teacher was not really listening—to either of them. He was caught in a turmoil of his own thoughts. That evening Father Pierre brought the Teacher and his friends to the meeting place of the untouchable people under the shade of the mango tree, and spoke to them about the school that was soon to be started.

"There must be many among you who may like to go," he said to us. "You have only to say so and these young people here would be glad to have you come."

To which the people made no answer then, but later, when the strangers had gone, they crowded round Father Pierre whom they knew and loved and trusted, and asked him many questions, voicing their many uneasy doubts.

"How can these things be?" they demurred. "Isn't the Acharya a Brahman?—aren't his companions people of caste?"

"In the eyes of God," Father Pierre answered them, "There is no Brahman and there is no Sudra. Neither is there any that may not be touched." Again and again he had said these words to them, times without number: yet again and again they asked; and he continued to answer them as ever he had done before, patiently, softly and gently, as if he were saying it to them for the first time.

He went on: "If men have looked upon you as untouchable, they have been wrong: no man is untouchable." In his firm and steady voice there were no doubts. There was a moment's silence. Then someone spoke, voicing his thoughts with painful slowness. "Swami, how can you say that? Always we have been the untouchable people. Our fathers and our fathers' fathers have been scavengers...and yet you say, Swami, that we are as other men are."

And the man who had spoken shook his head. His large simple face held in it no belief.

"Because a wrong is repeated ten thousand times, my brother, that does not make it a right," Father Pierre answered him gently. "Because for a thousand years a falsehood is repeated, that does not make it the truth.

Because for a thousand years men have called their brothers untouchable, that does not make them untouchable."

Linga said, "We are scavengers, are we not? Is not scavenging unclean work?"

Father Pierre answered gently: "Doesn't a mother gather the filth her child makes? Does that make her unclean?" They were silent then, but their brows were knotted and their eyes were troubled.

"Who will pay, master?" a man asked. "Who will pay for us to learn? What we earn cannot bring us enough for our bellies," he drummed upon his stomach with his fingers, "and what money can we give for our children to go to school?"

"The Acharya and his friends will take no money for teaching you," replied Father Pierre.

Soma broke in sharply, "And if they will take no money, why do they work? We may be untouchable and men may not touch us, but no man will refuse the money from our hands, for money cannot be polluted. Why do these people leave their homes and homesteads to come here and work if they will not take money?"

To that Kantanna reasoned gently: "Do you not remember they are Gandhi folk?"

Soma shrugged her shoulders and snorted. Her hard eyes held no belief, only mockery.

Several voices now repeated:

"Yes, they are followers of Gandhi."

"Ah," they all nodded, as if that explained it. "Ah," they murmured, to each other: "So they are Gandhi folk," and with this simple answer they were satisfied, and their doubts were stilled for a while.

"To the Mahatma all men are brothers as in truth they

are," said Father Pierre, but after a while another man began, speaking cautiously as if he were walking on the edge of a precipice.

"It is said that the Mahatma wishes to open the doors of the temple that we may enter, and worship before the image: is this true, Swami?"

"Yes, that is true," said Father Pierre.

"Are the temples he wishes to open like the Venugopala temple here?"

Father Pierre nodded. "The Venugopalapuram temple would be one of the many temples that would be opened to you."

"How can these things happen?" Linga broke in doubtfully again. "How would it be possible for us untouchable people to enter the temple? Are we not sweepers? Are we not untouchable? How can heaven-ordained things be changed even by the Mahatma?" And Ponchu looking at Father Pierre with her one eye, said: "For the sins of our past lives we have been born scavengers. Can the Mahatma erase what Brahma has written? And if he tried to open the doors of our sacred temples to the untouchables then who would eat the consequences of this sin? For isn't it a sin for an untouchable to pollute a Brahman?" So now they had come back to what they were saying in the beginning as if they had talked right round in a circle.

Father Pierre answered, again as gently and softly as if he was saying it for the first time: "In the sight of God no one is impure, no one is untouchable. In his sight all men are brothers."

But still they shook their heads, never completely convinced! "A Mahatma may do many things that ordinary people may not," they said, explaining away, as they always did, things which were outside the tradition.

Acharya Harishchandra's voice was not patient as Father Pierre's was. He spoke the same words but they burst from him with impatience and passion: "It would be better that the world and all things in it were shattered than that these things remained," he would shout, the blue veins swelling in his forehead. "Fools, fools, how—*when* will light dawn on you? Sometimes I wonder whose fault it is that you are sunk so low. Your chains are falling to pieces around you and you lift them up, and slip them upon yourselves again, as if they were rose garlands. You cannot live without them, it seems,"—When he spoke in anger a hush fell upon us all and we were cowed down with fear.

The girl Radha came to him then and said:

"Hold your temper, Harish! You will gain nothing in the end," while Father Pierre commented:

"Is it right to blame them for the sins that we have committed in our pride?" Soma listened to all this with a mocking smile on her lips.

One day the Acharya came into Father Pierre's hut when I was at work. Father Pierre had gone to attend to a woman who had coughed up blood. He had left me to look after the clinic and attend to people who came for medicines. Even before the Acharya came, I found myself thinking of him. My heart was singing; somehow I knew that he would come and I would see him, and suddenly I wished I were a beautiful girl. I did not know if I was beautiful. We scavengers do not think these thoughts, for it is a sin for untouchables to have thoughts about themselves. So I felt guilty and troubled, but nothing would remove the thoughts from me. I wished there was something in which I could see a reflection of myself and found it at last in the bell of Father

Pierre's bicycle which stood in a corner. I looked into it furtively, hoping my sin would not come to light, and all the while, I remember how my heart kept singing softly: "Am I beautiful? Am I beautiful?" I couldn't tell, though I looked for long into the little cycle-bell mirror. He came in as I was staring at my reflection and I started and grew confused at his sudden appearance. He said abruptly, standing in the doorway, stooping because it was so low and he was so tall:

"Is Father Pierre out?" and I answered that he was.

"Please sit down." I begged him. He came in and sat down. He seemed lost in thought, unaware that I was standing there near him, and I wondered if he could hear the pounding of my heart. He unfolded the newspaper in his hand, and began to read. It did not matter to him at all that I stood there and that my heart was bursting with love.

I gathered my courage. "My master," I whispered. But he did not seem to hear. So I moistened my dry lips, and spoke again, a little louder this time:

"My master?" and waited, still he did not look up. So I spoke again: "Master, may I do the scavenging in the school that the master has started?"

"Well, perhaps...we shall have to see." He bit his nails. "You see, girl, to be worthy of the cause I serve," he said "I must do the scavenging myself."

"Oh my master," I cried horrified, throwing up my hands in fear, "May the gods protect you. The master has caste, do not talk thus, my master! The three worlds will collapse before my master will do the work of a sweeper."

He shrugged his shoulders, and said:

"If I were true to the cause that I serve, then I would gather filth with you. Together we would carry the filth, girl. But I shall teach you and others like you to read and write and count, because that is nice, clean, respectable work, and then I shall set you to do the scavenging." There was anger hidden in his voice. But because he had spoken of ourselves together in one breath, it made me thrill with joy to hear him. Very timidly I asked him: "Are you angry, master?"

"H'm, yes," he said, "But not with you, girl," and added "You will come to the school, will you not?"

"My master, if you wish it, I will come," I answered.

But when I spoke to my mother about it she exclaimed: "The Acharya is a man of caste, daughter."

I answered, repeating what I had heard and longed to believe: "In the eyes of God there is no Brahman and there is no Sudra; neither is there any that may not be touched."

My mother stared at me, and my father put in sulkily: "And who will work while you sit among the twice-born people to learn the four Vedas and speak big words of wisdom? Who will earn the rice you eat, for it is rice that you must eat, is it not? Even a Brahman must eat rice to live; he cannot eat his books and knowledge!"

I answered instantly: "I will find the time—the school is only at night."

The untouchables quarter was agog with talk when my intention became known. "Oh gods in the heavens!" they exclaimed, "What is the world coming to, when an untouchable girl enters the home and school of a Brahman to sit alongside with him to learn the Scriptures?" Sometimes there was envy in the voices, sometimes anger, sometimes scorn, sometimes even joy, but always there was unbelief. Their words never reached me completely. With my ears I heard them speak; with my eyes I saw their faces. My lips smiled at them and sometimes uttered words in reply. But always the real me was elsewhere. I would hurry past them, and when I had left my broom and pan, I would take the earthen pitcher and make for the well, for my bath. I rubbed myself till my skin glowed. One day with my savings, I bought myself a sari. A second sari. My father muttered. "The girl grows too mighty for us. She bathes every day with soap. She buys new clothes for herself, she combs out her hair, she washes herself. When shall we see the end of all this?" He muttered these words, frowning darkly at me, eyes furtive and watchful. I did not answer. I had no fear of him; on the other hand I suspected that he, deep in his heart, feared me.

My mother murmured: "Still the girl earns more than anyone does. Father Pierre pays her besides, for helping with his medicines, and the Teacher will pay her for sweeping the school latrines." She began to count my earnings on her lean, knotty fingers, I wore my sari now with care. Hitherto it had always hung clumsily down, not covering my ankles. Now after my work I draped it lovingly around me making its folds neat and graceful. I began to notice with a secret joy how it clung to the new curves of my body.

Father Pierre had planted a jasmine creeper outside his hut. I began to gather its flowers and to string them for my hair. I made four little strings of jasmine. One I put before Mariamma's image, unfailingly; the second in my mother's tangled hair, the third I took to Sai or to Soma, and the one remaining last I put in my own braid.

After all this was done I would wonder timidly if the Teacher would notice the flowers in my hair. But he was busy with other things which were greater and more important. He never noticed the flowers in my hair or my beautiful new sari.

But if the Acharya did not notice, there were other people who did. One day when I walked in the Hanumanpura back lane with flowers in my hair, stones were thrown at me from back windows. I ducked and I missed being hit. I would have given it no thought knowing how children like to throw stones and do it carelessly, and unthinkingly, but angry voices called out after me: "Flowers in her hair...yes, flowers in her hair....What, what will she do next?" There were more stones. I fled from them and from their angry voices. I did not stop until I reached the untouchables' quarters, and was among my own kind.

"What happened?" Linga's wife asked me. "You look as if you were made of ash."

"Nothing..." I panted. "Nothing, mother. Nothing at all."

"Look at the flowers in her hair." Ponchu cried out. "What will she do next, eh, what will she do next? Flowers in her hair indeed as if she were a caste woman!"

I went to the Acharya's school. I learned to read and write, building on the foundation of Father Pierre's teaching. I sat with the children of the untouchable quarter, the tallest and oldest of them all and I worshipped the Teacher with all the intensity of my heart.

He spoke to us of a hundred things. In the beginning he was impatient with our slowness to understand, at our dull minds that would not absorb all that he taught. We would repeat after him whatever he said, but if he tried to make us unfold our own thoughts then he came up against a solid wall of silence. We had no answers to give him. His fists would clench then and the veins on his temples would throb and swell. But he would swallow his anger and force himself to speak gently. I was glad I could read and write already, even though I stumbled often.

When I had the time I would hurry to the shrine of Mariamma and there, after prostrating myself, I would sit down holding the book before me. My fingers would follow the words, my lips would move silently and I would read—at first a few words at a time, slowly, laboriously and then I must go over them again and put the words together to bring out their sense. I longed for his word of praise, for his nod of approval.

To read, to be able to read: these were new joys, but my greatest happiness remained in my Teacher. From where I sat on the stone slab floor of the school, my worshipping eyes gazed at him, never tiring, and I drank in his glorious beauty. My ears listened to the sound of his voice, and the smallest irritation in it I sensed, as well as the smallest note of pleasure, the least touch of weariness and dejection. He was my God, and in my heart I worshipped him. From him I asked nothing, hoped for nothing, sought nothing—but willingly and joyfully, I would have plucked my eyes from my face, if that had been required, to lay them at his feet in worship. I waited for him to speak and to smile. But he was stern most of the time, full of earnestness about his mission, for which his master sent him, and of the cause that he served. When he spoke outside the classroom he was brief and curt. Never did he speak of himself, neither of his family nor of his home in the city. When he spoke it was always about his work, and the work that must be done that would free our country.

He spoke passionately about the evil of foreign rule and as he spoke brought his clenched fists down upon the table. "But there are other evils, that we must fight," he said, "evils worse than the foreigners. These are evil enemies we nourish ourselves." He shot a finger at me and said:

"Tell me, girl, why do men call others untouchable? Why are you called untouchable—do you know?"

I reddened. My shyness was like a chain around me; I forced myself to answer. "Because, my master," I said under my breath, "Because we have been born as such." Then, gathering courage, I went on: "Our parents belong to the scavenging caste, as their parents did before them." It did not occur to me that there could be any other reason for a person's caste to be what it was, save his birth. If you asked a sheep why it was a sheep, what answer would it have except that it was because it had been born of sheep, who themselves had before it been born too, of sheep. In my mind I thought: "What a strange question to ask," and only because it was he that had asked it, I did not think it was a foolish one as well.

"Is that all that you have to say, girl?" he said, his voice irritated and impatient. "Can you not think? You have brains in your head, have you not? They are meant to think with. But sometimes I wonder if they are brains or is it straw?" His words hurt me, and I struggled with my tears:

"Go on—" he urged me, "Why have you been called untouchable?"

Struggling with my shame and mortification I answered: "Because my master, because—because—because we have sinned in our past lives." But even as I said this I knew he would not accept that for an answer.

"Enough, girl," he interrupted, shaking his head in despair. There was disappointment in his face, and I thought: "Oh, what a fool I am. Why does my black tongue not say what he wants me to say?"

"I will try to tell you what I think," said the Acharya. "You have been called untouchable only because you have allowed men to call you and treat you as such. You have allowed yourself to be treated worse than animals, and held out your hands for the shackles that men have put upon you. Time and again they told you that you were untouchable, and you, in your crass ignorance and simplicity believed it, and never questioned it. Do you understand? It is only because they have told you and your fathers that you are untouchable that you have believed it, and not because it is so. . . .But if you repeat a lie a hundred times over, does that make it the truth?"

I had no answer to that. Nervously I fidgeted with the slate pencil in my moist hands.

"Does it?" he asked, almost shouting. "Tell me, if a lie is repeated a thousand times over, does it cease to be a lie and become the truth?"

On my way home that evening I turned over and over the things he had said: "If a lie is repeated many times over, that does not make it the truth. A lie remains a lie. . ." and if I have been called an untouchable then that is a lie—I am no different from other human creatures—I am no different from the Acharya, the Teacher! But when I came to this point, a cold sweat ran down my face, and trickled down my back. And I had a frightening feeling as if I had suddenly been thrown into the air and left there with no support.

Just then Soma came sidling up and caught up with me. "What is it you're always thinking?" she wanted to know. I laughed unsteadily. The sound of her familiar voice was like the feel of the solid steady ground under my feet after the dizziness that had possessed me.

"You are always thinking—what do you think?" Soma laughed aloud. It was good to hear her laughter: we had come into the street that led to our homes.

"I have sugarcane," said Soma in her generous big way. "Take some." She held out a stick to me. I stripped it of its skin and broke a piece with my front teeth. Then chewing and spitting and chewing and spitting, we walked on.

"It is good sugarcane, very sweet and juicy and ripe." Soma chattered in her friendly way. "Take a piece each for your brothers and sisters. The poor chidren are thin and hungry," and she pressed the pieces into my hand.

"You are good to us, Soma," I said to her, but she waved her hand and only laughed.

"What do you think always?" she probed me growing serious, and I reddened with shame remembering my secret thoughts.

"How can I say, Soma, of what I think? One's thoughts come and go, do they not? And who can watch and remember thoughts?"

"H'm," Soma said: "Come, sit with me under the mango tree."

When we were seated together chewing the sugarcane, she said:

"The Teacher—the Acharya speaks to you, does he not?"

"Yes, he speaks to all." I answered. I kept my voice steady.

"Do you not find his words strange?" Soma gave me a sidelong, meaningful glance.

"How, Soma?" I asked, "In these times many people speak these words, do they not?"

"They speak them, yes. They repeat these words: words cost nothing to repeat. Everyone speaks and I am sick of their words."

I did not answer.

"And do you think that in their hearts they mean what they say?"

"Why—what—?" I stammered.

Soma's bright eyes grew very hard. She spat out the fibres of sugarcane.

"It is so easy to talk, to say, you and I, we are equal. We are alike. But is it so easy to live that way?—As if we were all equal—scavengers and tanners and cobblers and goldsmiths and temple priests. If we lived as if we were of one caste, if we lived with no barriers, with no divisions, then who would prevent me from being the wife of the temple high priest?"

"Why do you say these things to me, Soma," I asked unhappily. "What are these things to me?"

"Are they nothing to you?" Soma was laughing still. "If they are nothing, let them remain to you as nothing, Lachi, scavenger girl! Make no mistake! Words are like the husk of grain—empty, useless and plentiful. People give words, and that is all they have to give you." She pulled me up by my hand and we went down the street together. She laughed much as she walked and swayed her large hips and talked of many things—but I was silent and troubled, and full of guilt and fear that Soma had perhaps guessed my secret thoughts. But I could not help them. They filled my waking and sleeping hours.

The rains fell late that year. For many days the sky was hot with the sun's anger; white flames poured down to the earth and burnt the grass and left the river a thin muddy trickle. The water hole from which the untouchable people drew water dried up even earlier than it did each year. And the untouchable people went earlier this year for water at the well of the caste folk. They had done this in years past when the rains had been delayed. From our distance we would pray to the caste women for water.

"Rama!" the caste women would exclaim. "Must you eternally beg? Now it is money you ask, now clothes, now food! And now you come crying for water. It is the hot season, and the well would run dry with so many drawing from it. How much can we give, eh, how much? There is no end at all to your begging it seems! If you are given a finger, you try to swallow the hand!"

But though they spoke in this manner, some of them would come forward saying: "Leave your pots and go back. We will fill them for you." They would murmur to each other, shaking their heads sympathetically and rolling their eyes with kindness. "Who can live without water, sister, who can live? As we thirst, so do they, even the untouchables! To all men God has given hunger and thirst, even to the basest of his creatures. Even the scavenger folk!" Then the talk would turn to the greatness of God, His mercy, His limitlessness, and their hearts expanded with compassion. From our distance we scavengers caught their words as they talked. They poured out water for us holding themselves far from our pots, and we were deeply grateful; for what would we have done without water? This went on until there would come at last the day when the blazing sky would grow close and heavy with the haze of the heat. And one day towards evening the wind would rise suddenly, and squall over the land; the clouds would heave and roll. Lightning and thunder would rend them and suddenly burst forth on every side, and the earth would be fragrant with the smell of rain. But this year the rains did not come. The sun grew hotter and the earth was like a furnace. And because water was scarce and people thirsty, goodwill and friendliness began to crack under the strain. At the well of the caste-people where the women gathered, there were quarrels now and unpleasantness and hard words among them, and screaming women flung stones at the untouchable people who approached the spot for water.

One day the wife of the temple cook saw the untouchables waiting and cried out in a vicious voice: "There they come, all dressed like queens!"

The scribe's mother-in-law clapped her hand on her forehead: "Ayya!" she cried, her voice thick with sarcasm, "All these years there was one thing that had been left undone, the pollution of the drinking-water well. Now the day has dawned when that too must be done and then we shall have peace and salvation! Here they come then. Surely my sisters, we must make way that they may go and pollute the water!"

Angry voices shouted angrily to us: "Stand back hussies...Have you no shame?" Gathering courage I ventured: "We beg for water, mother—the water hole of the untouchables is dry."

"Indeed! And this one? Do you think this brims over with rain water?"

The temple cook's wife took up: "If you ask why, then I will tell you. It is because it is an age of sin, Kali Yuga, when castes mix and cause confusion and chaos. There's a drought, which the gods have sent in anger and how can we give water when we haven't any for ourselves?"

A sad-eyed woman said: "I will pour out some for you, children. Wait till I fill my pitcher."

The wrath of the women turned upon her. "Aha. So you will, will you? Do so, do so by all means, only remember you will give them from your share of water, no more—not a drop more will you draw."

The woman drew in a swift breath, and her companions continued: "They have their own well of water. Why do they come here?"

"It is dry. The girl says it is dry," the sad-eyed woman answered.

"How can we help that?" an old widow demanded. "If their well is dry, sister, are we to blame? Is it our fault or is it their misfortune? Isn't it the fruit of their past sins? Of past selfishnesses and untruths and greeds, of their karma of past lives?"

The other woman said in a soft voice:

"Surely then if we deny thirsty people a share of water we too shall reap the fruit of it in lives to come." That made the women even angrier.

"Ayya, ayya. Here we thirst in the rainless summer heat, and she talks high philosophy for our benefit!" they cried.

"Thirst is not quenched nor the belly filled with big words of knowledge, Satyabhama!" they hissed at her. And then they shouted to us: "Go from here now. In this well there is no water, there is very little."

Soma said defiantly: "I will look and see. I can't believe that the well is dry." She went round walking with her swaggering gait. Leaning over the parapet she peeped into the well.

"Rama! oh, Rama, Rama!" the women screeched. "She touched the well. Polluted, polluted. For shame! Help."

Soma shrugged her shoulders, and said coolly: "There is water enough in the well for all of us," as if she had not heard their cries at all.

"Fouled! Polluted!" they continued to scream. "She has touched the well! The drinking-water well has been fouled by a scavenger. Ayyo, Rama! Rama!" They surrounded her like wild cats.

"Let us go! Oh, let us go!" Sai said close to my ear.

I answered her: "We cannot now. They are all round us.

Do not be afraid." But for all my brave show, I felt my fear twist and turn within me.

Soma said to them in her insolent voice: "I need to drink water as much as you do, good mothers. As you thirst, so do I too. And there is water in this well. How can you prevent me from drawing it, eh? What will you do to me? What will you do?" And she stood before them, in her usual attitude of insolence and defiance. They flung abuse and curses at her. They were all talking together and gesticulating.

"Come Soma! Have you lost your reason?" I asked Soma. But Soma tossed her head and gave me a scornful glance.

"Was not water made for all?" she went on. "Else why do all people thirst alike?"

The passers-by collected to watch. Tempers flared up once more, as the story of the fouling of the water well was, at each turn, repeated for their hearing. When we saw the junior priest of the temple pushing forward in the crowd, adding his voice to the medley of voices, Soma began to laugh, and Sai bit her lip, and caught my hand. Her fingers were cold and moist with fear, and she moved behind Soma, with a sudden, quick movement.

I said again, persuasively, "Do not be afraid, Sai. Words are only words after all and they cannot really hurt us."

The junior priest asked in his squeaky voice: "What has happened?" They repeated the story for him, breathless with anger and emotion, pointing to Soma and screaming hysterically: "There she stands, the slut who fouled the well. What shall we drink through the summer? Oh, evil day! Oh, our fate! Oh! this sinful, sinful age."

The priest turned to Soma: "Scavenger girl," he leered at her, "surely you could have asked for water. You could have begged and they would have given it to you. Why did you have to touch the well and foul it?"

She shrugged her shoulders. Her arched eyebrow lifted and her lips curled. Turning only her head sideways to look at him she said, quite softly and yet so that all could hear: "Pollution, my master! Pollution! you speak of Pollution to me?".... And she laughed. He turned from her quickly. His voice was nervous as he said to the women: "If she has fouled the well, my mothers, it can be purified again. The scavenger folk themselves shall pay for its purification. Never fear. Stop cackling, women, and go home now. Today the high priest himself shall purify the well. For him it is not a big matter."

The women were murmuring still. But their voices were lower now. The priest had assured them and they were glad of the excuse to put an end to the scene without loss of face. They went away muttering and mumbling, throwing hate-filled looks in our direction.

"Let us go, Soma!" I whispered. "Oh, let us go."

The junior priest was eyeing me and his look made me tremble.

"Why are you afraid, you little mouse?" Soma sneered. She turned to the priest, the remains of the sneer in her voice still: "Swami!" she said, "Can you pour out water for us?"

"Your impudence passes all telling, does it not?" he said.

"Give us water, swami, give us water." Soma laughed. "Fill our pitchers." He flung an angry look at her, but there was only amused contempt in her eyes. Muttering and cursing, the junior priest poured out water into our pots, and Soma smiled mockingly as he did so.

The summer wore on, each day hotter than the last. Still the rain had not come. At the water well there were angry scenes every day, now fights and clamourings. The caste women threatned the untouchables with dire things if they came. But many of the untouchables continued to go, nevertheless, following Soma, for there was no other course open to them. With their pitchers and pots and empty tins they went and waited, deaf to the curses flung at them. Sometimes they went at midnight, silently, fearfully like ghosts, and drew water from the well. And because their need was so great they brushed aside the fear of the sin they committed in fouling the water well and stealing water. The brawls grew into angry fights—stones were flung, and the policemen came with sticks.

On the fifth day as we were approaching the well, we saw there the familiar figures of Father Pierre and of the Acharya and his friends. They stood near the well, and faced the caste women. There was a babel of voices as usual. The women were talking all together. The Acharya and his friends were making vain attempts to speak and be heard. I could see him hold up his hand, appealing for silence. The women were pointing vicious fingers at him and screaming. But after a while the Acharya suddenly leaped on the well's rim and shouted very loudly so that there was a startled silence and all the women turned towards him: "There is wrong being done here, my friends, gross injustice and sin. The scavenger folk need water as much as anyone else does, and to deny water to a thirsting fellow is a grave wrong."

"Get out from here, idler, vagabond!" a woman shouted from the crowd. "Who are you to tell us?"

"He wants to destroy our heaven-ordained laws—he wants to defy the gods—."

Acharya Harishchandra said: "There's wrong being done at the water well. But the Mahatma says wrong cannot be answered by wrong. Injustice cannot be wiped away with more injustice, sin cannot overcome sin. These things, says the Mahatma, can only be righted by penance and suffering, suffering even to the point of death. So we who claim to be his followers and walk in his footsteps, we must do his bidding. And that is why my friends, Govinda and Ramakrishna, and I, we three, have declared our intention to take upon ourselves this penance. Twenty four hours from now we intend to begin a fast to atone for the sin committed at the well?"

There was a sound of breaths swiftly drawn in. " Fast? Fast?" We gazed at him with frightened eyes: "Fast for the scavengers, the untouchables?"

"Not untouchables," Father Pierre pointed out. "Not untouchables but the children of God—Harijans."

"A fast." said Acharya impatient at the interruption. "A fast unto death—!"

Squatting among my people, listening to these words, I felt my body grow chill and numb. I shivered, and forgot all things except one thing, that he whom I worshipped would be in danger of death, and I was desperate at the thought. All other things vanished from my mind and I no longer remembered water for my thirsting people, or caste and untouchability, wrongs and injustices: all these fell away from me. Only one thought remained away in my mind: "If he should die, Oh, if he should die, if he should bring death upon himself!"

"They have thought carefully about this for days." Father Pierre told us, "While you have been at the water well, their minds have been looking for some answer other than the answer of blood and hate. The way of Satyagraha seems to them the only way."

And at that point I heard myself crying out wildly: "No—no—no!"

The people turned their eyes on me, but I was sobbing: "No—no—no—he cannot go to his death. He must not, not even for our thirst." I had covered my face with my hands. Father Pierre stepped over to me and began to draw me away. "What have we to do with fine words?" I cried out rebelliously and loudly. "How can we let him die?"

"Come, child," Father Pierre said. "Come into the house." So he led me away, and in his hut he gave me a little cool water from the earthen drinking-water pot to wash my face and swollen eyes.

I wept when I thought of the Acharya going to fast for our sake. Soma laughed at me, and called me a silly creature. "Do you think this man has seen your tears?" She asked me: "Child, if you drowned yourself in your tears for him, still he would not know, and it would not matter to him. Don't you see he is one of them?" There was bitter hatred in her voice when she pronounced the word "them". I answered nothing at all and Soma went on: "You are foolish, girl. What do you think you are getting, or seeking?"

"Nothing!" I answered in a small voice, "I seek nothing. Still I—I do not want him to die."

"And what would you gain if he lived?" Soma persisted. "What would it matter to you if he died or lived?"

"Do not pester me, Soma," I begged, but Soma went on as if she had not heard: "Listen foolish one," she said, her voice grave now with warning, "I do not know why I speak to you and tell you these things, but I do. A one-sided love is bitter and barren and there is Mada who is betrothed to you.

It is not every girl that has a man as good as Mada is. His face is like a sheep's—true, and he does not have beautiful words or learning but he will make you a good husband. What is there between you and this Teacher? What can there ever be? Do not mistake me. Between us and them there is the whole earth and words will not span the distance."

I knew she was speaking the truth, and told her so.

"If you know it then why do you waste yourself?" Soma cried, gripping my shoulder.

"I told you, already" I answered desperately, "I told you, I want nothing. It is only inside me, somewhere, that I have thoughts—and dreams, which I cannot help."

Soma sneered at this: "Where will all this take you, fool? For how long will you follow a dream? Chase a shadow? Tell me that—how long?"

As we walked slowly we noticed a crowd of people approaching. They were on the way to the well, where the Gandhi men were to speak in a little while. At the well there was a tense crowd. The anger of the crowd was near the surface, but had not burst forth yet. The Acharya was speaking: "Do you not see," he was saying, "that what you are doing is wrong. And will not the ghosts of those to whom you denied water come to you and reproach you? Water is for all people. Can you write your name upon water to say 'This is mine and no one else may touch it?' When a scavenger touches it, does water change its colour or nature? When the rain falls, does it not rain alike on me and you and on the man who cleans the latrines? Is the rain polluted? Are the clouds in the heavens defiled?"

A voice answered from the crowd: "It is easy to talk, young man—but—through the ages, we have followed the law laid down by men wiser than you and me. And now has it come to this that we must hear the law interpreted by boys like you, to have to stand and watch while you break down what the ancients built?"

The crowd began to grow restive. There were murmurings: "Once this starts where will it end? The accumulation of sin will grow from a mound to a hillock to a mountain and the earth itself will be crushed under its weight."

They were growing angry, and their faces were dark and taut. But the Teacher's eyes were quiet; his voice unruffled. He called them his brothers and sisters. He continued to speak, to exhort them, plead with them: "The laws were made by the ancients for their own times," he said. "But those times have gone. For that world of other years and for those times the laws no doubt were just and good."

A shout came from the crowd, jeering and sarcastic: "Yes, yes, crouch at his feet and listen!"

The Teacher's lips tightened into a line for a second and his eyes shot fire. A lock of hair fell on his forehead; he brushed it impatiently aside. But when he spoke, his voice continued unruffled: "Time is like a never-ending river. If we block its course with the accretions of the days, there will come a day when it will burst its banks, and overflow and bring destruction. The world we live in is like a crumbling edifice. If we do not rebuild it, it will collapse upon us, and we will all be crushed beneath it."

"Ayya!" someone shouted. "He talks now in riddles because it sounds more learned. Why do you come talking? If you wish, go yourself and marry a sweeper-girl, but why do you come prating to us?"

"I come prating to you, because there...." But he never finished what he had begun to say. Angry voices interrupted him: "Get out from here. Out!" and the crowd advanced on him menacingly.

"Are you trying to cow us down into submission? To bend us with this rod into letting the untouchable people foul our drinking water, and soil our sacred threads for ever? What new mischief is this?"

"It is not mischief," the Acharya answered, "We want nothing but to take upon ourselves the burden of the wrong that we commit each time we spit upon our brother and call him foul."

"Take them away," voices shouted, "remove them."

The Teacher went on—"What we are doing is what we believe to be the truth. For the sake of this truth we must face all things—even death."

Two angry men came up and faced them. They began to shake their fists: "Enough!" they shouted, "Babbler, fatherless one! Who was your mother, ai, who?"

And then the crowd began to heave. The men surrounded the four who stood at the well, advancing in a rush in their fury. They did not see us, untouchables, or perhaps having seen, they did not care. They brushed past us and approached the Gandhi men.

"Beat them! They come preaching at us! And tomorrow they will ask us to give our daughters in marriage to untouchables: we will teach them! We will show them! Satyagraha! Huh!"

Shouting, screaming, they lifted the men from where they stood. The demons in them set to work as they hit and pounded and kicked them without mercy. There was a riot; I was praying frantically, saying only again and again. "Mariamma! Oh Mariamma! Have mercy. Oh ye gods have mercy!" I did not care what happened to all the world. Only him I did not want hurt. Not a hair of his head could I have borne to see hurt. So I called to Mariamma for mercy.

But often Mariamma is deaf like stone. And the Teacher

was hurt. His face was a mass of blood. I saw him reel, bleeding. I saw someone catch him, and when I ran to the spot I saw it was Radha. Radha called to the crowd to move. Her voice had command in it, and the people hearing her fell back to make place. She sat down by the well-side with the Acharya's head in her lap, and I saw Father Pierre was also near by.

Father Pierre said: "Bring water, child," briefly. From among the pitchers ranged by the well-side I grabbed one, and I fastened the rope to its neck, and let it down fast into the well. I drew water, and brought it to him where he lay with his head on Radha's knee, blood streaming down his face. I knelt down and moistened his lips with the water.

They took him away on a stretcher. The police had come by then, and the people fell back to ward off their blows, but many were hurt, though none so badly as the Teacher.

They carried him to Father Pierre's hut where he lay in a twilight of half-consciousness. I stood at the door weeping. My heart cried out to Mariamma to save him, not to let him die. I made a vow that if he should recover, I would sacrifice a sheep at Mariamma's shrine and offer up flesh and blood to appease the Goddess' hunger. But when I told this to Soma, to get her help and advice she looked at me and said scornfully:

"You will rue it! A sheep? Are you mad? Who will pay for it? Where will the money come from? And this man that you are crying your heart out for, tell me, what does he have to do with us?"

All she said was perhaps true, but at that time, full of the brave words that were in the air, I was like one drunk with strong wine. I only saw that which I wanted to see, and a hope fluttered in my heart that our worlds were not so far apart as Soma made them out to be.

"Where will the money come from, fool?" Soma asked.

"I will go to the Settis," I answered without flinching. She laughed.

"You are a fool—Do you think you will be given the money because you ask for it? What have you to offer as a security?"

"I have nothing," I answered humbly.

Soma said brusquely: "You are a fool, your head is empty as a scooped out gourd!"

"What can I do? This is how I was made." I said. In Soma's presence I always felt small, insignificant and foolish.

"You are like a stupid fish which swallows the bait and allows itself to be caught and cooked," she went on in a vicious voice and I nodded even more humbly. She laughed loudly. "You will have your sheep, fool; I will get one for you." I was dumb with gratitude. "And you can pay me when you can," she said, when she had finished laughing. "It will be offered to the Goddess in the place of the Acharya's blood."

I could only gasp at that, stupefied by her big careless generosity.

The Teacher lived. One day he opened his eyes and spoke and I knew that the goddess had accepted my offering and heard my prayer. Father Pierre said, "He will recover," and in my heart was happiness, and gratitude to the goddess.

Radha was arrested. She was taken away and put in jail. Secretly, though I knew it to be wicked, I felt relieved and happy that she was not there. It was I who sat now beside him during the day, and who by night slept on the floor, springing up at the smallest sigh or sound or movement from him. Oh, I was in a transport of bliss! He began to recover and to regain his strength. He began to look about him with the light of recognition in his eyes. He began to speak, to call me by my name. He bade me sit down and to read to him, or speak to him, and the happiness in my heart swelled till I felt I could not bear the sweet pain of it. I had suddenly set my foot in a new heaven and its doors had swung open for me and I had walked into its light. And all that the saints had taught and all that Father Pierre had said came back to me: In the eyes of God, my heart sang in exultation, there is no Brahman and there is no Sudra. Neither is there any that may be called untouchable.

But time will not stand still and other things took place in my life during those days and one of them was my mother's passing. She had been ill for many months, losing blood and her face had grown grey as ash.

"There are not many more days for me to live," she said often to Ponchu. "My days are passed, and now I am like a leaf cup from which the food has all been emptied." Ponchu would try to cheer her. "What are you saying? Let the children grow and give you grandchildren. Never fear—you will live yet for many days." But my mother smiled faintly and said: "It is all over...I have lived out the hours I brought with me."

During the days that followed, however, there was a sudden lull in the course of her illness, and she seemed better; she seemed slowly to grow stronger, and was able to sit where once she lay, and her grey withered face flushed with new colour. Ponchu said to me: "Come child, come, come home and feed your mother gruel and moisten her lips," and I went, but with heavy feet. I did what was needed of me but the minutes I spent away from the sunshine of the Acharya's presence seemed too long. I grudged them. Father Pierre came to see my mother. He pricked her with his medicine needles. "Perhaps at the hospital—," he began. But my mother would not go to the hospital, and told Father Pierre so with joined hands and tears. A fortnight dragged by, and one day, when I was away sitting with the Acharya, my father came into the hut full of liquor and anger and abuse and threats, and demanded money from his wife. There was no money to give him, and so as he had always done, he fell upon her that day and dragging her from where she lay, spat on her and beat her. And then, when his fury was spent, he threw her on the floor and strode away. She was lying there in a daze when I came home at last. She was lying writhing and groaning on the floor. I lifted her and carried her to her mat and laid her on it. Remorse overcame me and fear, because I had forgotten her in my own happiness. It was getting dark. I lit the tin oil lamp and looked at the smoke curling upwards. My brothers sat in a corner covered with a blanket, their knees drawn up to their chests. My mother lay in a stupor, muttering from time to time, and mostly she was haunted by dreams of her first-born, her Boda who had gone from her. Once she stared at me with strangely luminous eyes. She half rose in her bed pointing at some distant object and began to scream disjointedly and incoherently:

"My daughter, stay away—stay away! It is the idol in the temple that you defile with your touch."

The lamp flickered and snuffed itself out, for the oil was low, but a ray of pale moonlight from the waning moon fell into the room through the hole in the wall. After a while my mother's raving ceased suddenly, and she grew quiet and still, but now Nagi began to whimper; so I fed her gruel from the earthen pot, and rocked her to sleep holding her against my body. I wished that Father Pierre would come, but he was away in Kolampet. All grew quiet again. My brother fell asleep, and I sat by my mother listening to her heavy breathing.

She died in the night. I was sitting with her, and Nagi was in my arms. My eyes were heavy and in my half-asleep and half-awake state dreams came to me forming and reforming themselves and vanishing for a while, and when I thought they were gone, they arose again in fantastic weird forms. When I tried to grapple with them, they were empty air. I seemed to hear voices and echoes, muffled by the mists and the clouds, all calling my name. I started and woke to find it was my mother calling my name. She had raised herself and was staring: "It is the Goddess, it is Mariamma, the Goddess," she was whispering: "Oh, my mother, have you come then?" She stretched out her wasted hands. The light in my mother's face frightened me, and I cried out, "Mother, my mother," but she sank back, her breath suddenly changing into wheezing sounds. I caught her in my arms and laid her head upon my lap. She seemed to be looking for something around the dimly lit room. But after a second her eyes returned, disappointed, to rest on my face; her lips moved, "My mother, Mariamma, is that you, come at last? And so whispering, life left her.

I held her withered hands, dry as straw, and I was tearless with loneliness and grief. Tearlessly I smoothed back the wisps of hair from her forehead. I sat there for a long, long time, my mind unable to understand anything. It was crying out, "Why, why," in a distracted sort of way; for everything seemed so utterly, utterly devoid and empty of meaning.

Nagi was crying, woken suddenly from her sleep. The

boys woke, and looking at me they staggered up, their eyes wide-open and scared. "Go for Granny Ponchu," I said to them, and they stole away, while I sat still holding the body. Ponchu came in to wail and as the morning broke, all the women in the quarters also came. All wept and wailed as was the custom, sitting around the body, beating their breasts and singing the songs of death and of mourning.

Ponchu said the body must be washed, and that I must do it. Then I must dry it and wrap around it a saffron-coloured sari, because a woman who has died unwidowed and smiling, must be borne away like a bride. I must adorn the stiff dead face with vermilion and turmeric; and place flowers in the hair, and tulsi leaves in various parts of the body. Now that she was dead she could be adorned with the flowers. The women of the scavenger quarters clustered around me while I did these things, singing the songs of a woman's death. When all was finished the men came with the bier, festooned with marigold, bougainvilleas and scarlet hibiscus. My father was with them. They had found him drunk on the street. There was someone else too, who had come: it was the Teacher, the twice-born Acharya. When the men lifted the bier, the Acharya gave his shoulder wordlessly, and helped to carry the body away. My father was drunk and raving. He wept loudly, and tore his hair. As they approached the scavengers' burial ground he broke suddenly into the funeral dance, the tears streaming down his face. He danced thus, going before the bier of the dead, all the way to the burial place. When they came back it was as if my mother had never been. There was nothing to tell that once she had existed, had spoken and moved and smiled and wept, and walked upon the earth. Death had swallowed all. Already the weeping and wailing of the women had ceased, and the children stole away. Only I remained in the hut sitting in the corner, my chin resting on my drawn-up knees, my eyes staring before me.

They carried her away with the music of pipes and kettle drums and the singing of women. All these had to be paid for and I wondered what we had to pawn. A few pots and pans, tattered clothing. My anklets and earrings and my nose-ring. They would fetch a little and pay for the funeral. There would have to be a feast afterwards.

When Father Pierre returned the next morning I began to weep. "Perhaps if you had been here, Swami, she would not have died."

"Dear child," he answered, "I had to go. It happened very suddenly. I hurried here as soon as I heard. But she was tired and ill and in pain with the cancer eating at her vitals. Only God could give her rest and freedom. I am a poor mortal, and I could have done nothing for her. Do you not see she will never more suffer pain?" I nodded, the tears slipping from my eyes nevertheless. I put my hands to my face and wept.

"You are right, my father, I understand, and yet, and yet, if you had been here, she might not have gone."

He was very kind to me. Perhaps if he had been there my mother would not have died then. And perhaps, if Father Pierre had been with us he could have saved Kittu today.

Friends and relations come to visit me and weep with me for Kittu. They squat ouside the hut and they wail and sing over and over again the songs of mourning. Sometimes they dance to show their grief, just as they had done during the ten days after my mother had gone.

A feast had to be given for my dead mother's soul, or

else, they told me, her spirit would be hungry and would return to trouble me. All the people who had come to visit us and mourn with us had to be fed or the dead woman's soul would have no peace. Her unappeased ghost would enter the bodies of living people and cause disease and madness.

And so we must get rice and provisions to feed the people so that my dead mother's hunger would not haunt us.

Kittu died in the flower of his youth. All must be fed or Kittu's soul too will have no peace, and his ghost will haunt you.

"Where will the money come from?" I wondered. I had asked that question before when we returned from my mother's funeral.

"The Setti on Temple Street," Ponchu had said to me, and I went with her. He was a shining, black man, potbellied and podgy like the Elephant God with rings glinting and sparkling on his fat fingers. His son sits there now, for the old Setti is dead. Today too I approach the shop for provisions for the funeral feast for Kittu, and the Setti looks as his father did—shining, pot-bellied, Elephant God, with small sharp eyes.

We, the untouchable may buy, but we must stand at a distance, or else there will be trouble. When we have no money the man gives us credit. He enters all the moneys lent out in a long ledger book and he calculates and explains to us from time to time the reason why our debts rise and rise until we are drowned in them. It is the interest, he explains. The interest doubles and redoubles itself until we cannot keep count at all, but have to rely on the Setti's knowledge of figures and their calculation. The interest is like iron shackles on our feet and they chain us to him for ever and ever and there is no escape.

"You must go to the Setti. Only he will be able to lend you money enough." said Ponchu to me in the days of mourning for my mother. Custom is a tyrant and will offer no other course. We must do what has always been done. There is no escape. So we went to the Setti, Soma and I. And Soma got for me the money I needed. She smiled at the Setti and fluttered her eyes at him and winked and laughed and the Setti grimaced at her and stroked the loose folds of his stomach with his beringed fat hands, and laughed and joked and agreed to lend a sum of fifty rupees and the interest was half a rupee on every rupee borrowed. "It is a favour I do," said the Setti.

"But not for nothing," snapped Soma laughing. She would not speak as we walked back home.

What have I done? I have borrowed again for Kittu's funeral and funeral feast. My earnings, our needs, our daily rice, all our future I have pawned to the Setti for Kittu's funeral feast. Everything spins madly around me and I leave off calculating. For so many days we had somehow managed to be free. And while Kittu was alive, we had fed on gruel and ground chillies. But now that he is dead there must be a feast and I have walked now into the pit and there is no escape. And it was the same when my mother died. "That is the way it is," Ponchu had said then when I took my worry to her. "That is the way it always has been. No one can live alone. All are bound, one to another, by shackles. The Setti is as much a part of our lives as anyone else."

It did not worry her overmuch, for there was no escape and there never had been. She did not look for one, for that was the way it was.

———

I was waiting one day for my share of water by the well of the untouchable people, when I saw a figure walking slowly down the lane towards the scavengers' quarters. He advanced, tottering as if drunk, making for a tree. He held out his hands; when he neared the tree he caught it and sank under it. It took me a while to recognise the man to be my brother, Boda. Then I let my waterpot fall to my feet, and I ran to him, calling him. He did not look up. His head had sunk on his chest. He was groaning as if in pain. I called his name, several times before he opened his eyes and stared at me, as if he did not remember.

"Boda, my brother, my brother!" I cried. In that instant I knew how much I had missed him in my life.

"Why, it is Lachi," Boda's eyes brightened briefly. Then they went dead.

"What has happened?" I asked. "Are you hurt, my brother?" He had become very thin. The eyes had sunk into their sockets, and the cheeks had caved in. His arms and legs were like bamboo sticks. He was wearing city clothes—a shirt and a pair of knee-length trousers. His hair was red with travel dust.

"Come, come home, Boda." Taking him by the hand I led him home. People recognised him as we went.

"It is Boda," they cried, and came running up. "How thin he has grown!"

Ponchu came hobbling up: "Vagabond, fatherless one, why did you go from us? Your mother died weeping her heart out for you. Shame on you to have thrown ashes on the belly that gave you birth." But though she scolded and cursed, Ponchu was truly happy at his return. She pressed her gnarled hands on his chin and cracked her knuckles upon her temples and said after a while:

"You have come at last, and it does my heart good to see you. May Mariamma protect you, child. May Mariamma keep you and bless you!"

"Why did you go, my brother?" I asked him. "Granny Ponchu is right. Our mother lived her days yearning for you, and when she died her desire remained. Why did you go?"

"How could I stay here?" Boda answered, "and work in filth and be called untouchable and treated worse than a pig. How could I stay? What was there for me here? It is water perhaps that runs in your veins, girl, but I have blood in mine."

"You were no worse than we were," I ventured, but he turned angry eyes upon me.

"Leave it now, let us not talk of it any more," I said hastily. "It is good that you have come. Oh it is good to see you again." Then I told him of our mother's death. He listened with his ears, but I do not think his mind took in my words or their meaning. "Our mother is dead, but I will look after you, and I will feed you, Boda," I promised. He was ill with fever. He lay on the floor of the hut and cried out in pain and delirium and for many days we were not sure whether he would live or die. He had a racking cough, and even after the fever left him the cough remained. He sat for many hours brooding moodily outside the hut, and had nothing but sullen glances for the people who came to see him.

No, Boda was not like my son Kittu. My Kittu was full of laughter and hope, and Kittu's face was open and radiant like the full moon. But Boda brooded and cursed under his breath, and had nothing but anger for the people around him. He had not changed.

My father continued to curse him: "Why did you come? Why did you not stay where you were?" he often asked bitterly. He said to me:

"Who will feed this prince and godling? Who will feed him rice?"

"I will if you won't. . . ." I said, "and if you beat him or abuse him I will leave this roof and go."

My father sat down to eat, and Boda sat outside, on the earth, leaning against the mud wall, smoking and spitting and answered nothing. For all Boda said or cared the man might not have been there at all.

Boda lived with us, but he was not one of us. He had nothing to say to the children, and towards our father he remained indifferent and contemptuous. He sat in the doorway and smoked and chewed tobacco in betel leaf and spat all around him. Sometimes he went down to Venugopalapuram in his city clothes and returned with more beedies and tobacco and betel leaf. He did not work, not even in the house, but I didn't complain of this for I could see that he had been ill. Sometimes he was seized with spells of coughing and then he spat out, and in his sleep he groaned, and his fever returned to him often. Father Pierre, came and saw him and spoke to him of the city and of the sights he had seen. But even to Father Pierre, Boda had no friendly words to say.

But there were times when he would speak to me and unburden himself. Over a period of time he told me of his life in the city after he had gone from Venugopalapuram. Sometimes he spoke just a sentence or two, sometimes he sat down and told his story for over an hour. He did not tell the story in the order that it happened, but I put the fragments together and I lived his experiences, as if they had happened to me. He told me how he had walked the six miles between our home and the Venugopalapuram railway station and had entered the train unseen from the track, and travelled to Bombay. The train travelled for two days and a night, and Boda sat on the floor of the compartment. He had bought himself a ticket with money he had secretly saved from his earnings. And Soma had given him some, he said, "Go break the bars of your prison and go out and be made whole." Soma had told him. "I would come with you if I could." But he could not persuade her though he tried. She walked with him to the railway station.

"Perhaps a new life will open out to you in the city," she told him. "Go, go when you are young and strong."

During the journey Boda lay low and did not speak to anyone. For all his bravado, now that he was alone, in a strange new place, he felt nervous and small. His tongue and lips grew dry when he thought of the unknown future before him.

"O Mariamma!" cried Boda who had never before prayed. "O Mariamma, protect me." And once or twice he thought he would turn and run back. But again his heart said: Run back to be called untouchable. Run back to the scavenger's existence. And he set his teeth and told himself that come what may, he would break his prison bars. He would live as a human being, among human beings. In the city, they said, one's caste did not matter. Working hands were needed and if you worked you ate. Boda wondered whether this was really true. It seemed true, for in the train no one asked him his caste. The compartment was crowded with people. Some of the men were talking and discussing loudly the news of the day, especially Gandhi, the Mahatma, and his fight with the British for Independence. He could not understand all that they said, but one thing he heard them say again and again: "Independence, yes—but Gandhi is going too far. Are we to sit on the same level as scavengers and tanners, and be ruled by pariahs and sweepers? Gandhi does not understand what he is doing, what forces he is letting loose when he talks as he does. He puts ideas into people's heads, stirs up trouble and danger." Boda felt sick with the rocking movement of the train. His head reeled and ached. Bits of coal flew into his eyes, and his mouth felt foul and bitter. But as time passed his fear grew less and the sense of adventure continued to stir his blood: the world seemed to unroll itself before him and for him. He sensed an uneasiness in the people who were talking. Times were changing. For him things would be different when he reached the city.

My Kittu never reached the city. Death was walking beside him and it overtook him before he reached the railway station. All is fate, and no one can cheat fate or escape destiny. But to die as my boy Kittu did—was it some sin that he had committed in his previous life? Or some fearful things that I had done in some unremembered existence? Is this the retribution that has been justly meted out to us? I have no answers to the questions that wheel about in my mind.

Boda reached the city. He was tired and sore, and the vomiting and giddiness had eaten into his vitals. The train ground to a stop at last. But Boda lay in a stupor on the floor of the compartment.

"Ass, and son of an ass," someone bellowed, "This is Bombay. This is the Bori Bunder station, don't you see?"

Boda got out, his head reeling, his legs unsteady under him. In a blur he saw crowds of people, hundreds and thousands of people, countless numbers of people, swarming about him. He stood open-mouthed, not knowing what to do, where to go. People brushed past him, jostled him, walked over his shadow. Many, many hands touched him. But no one looked at him or noticed him at all. They walked as if they were all intent on some mysterious far-away goal—as if driven towards it by some terrible unseen force.

"Where is my untouchability gone?" Boda wondered, and looked at his arms and hands. They had not changed. He felt uneasy and his legs shook.

"Move on, move on," a porter shouted, "Why do you stand in the way gaping?"

He began to walk with the streams of people, one of the crowds. He showed his ticket at the gate and came out with the people. On the road were many motor cars. There were great buses, bigger than elephants and clanking boxes on wheels attached to wires above and carrying crowds of people. And no one looked at him or noticed him or recognised his untouchability. No one moved away from him. No one cried out in warning: no one shied away from his shadow. Suddenly he became very frightened at this, but he steeled himself and gathered up his courage. He had a few coins. He bought himself a measure of roasted gram and cup of hot tea. He ate and drank, standing alongside people whom he did not know and who did not know him. They did not look at him or ask him his caste. And he saw now that people were right when they said that in the city a man's caste did not matter at all. But all the same inside him his uneasiness continued. He had come to escape from the prison of untouchability, but the prison would not leave him and presently the thought of his untouchability began to torment him as it had never before done. Again and again he found himself wondering if he was not unwittingly committing a heinous sin by polluting so many people.

He stepped into the street. It seemed bigger than the

whole town of Venugopalapuram. He began to walk. Because he did not know anyone or any street, one place was as good to him as another. He was a stranger everywhere. Several times he was nearly run over, and killed by the cars, and the clanking moving boxes on rails. (Later he learned that these boxes were called tramcars.) The drivers of the vehicles shouted abuses and spat at him, crying, "Do you want to die, lout?"

He walked on and on until suddenly he came to the end of the road, and before him was water and great ships stood out in the sea. Nearer, by the edge, boats were anchored. Boda saw large numbers of men carrying from them heavy wooden boxes and sacks. He stood watching the men as they worked. In the evening the lights came out on the streets and the shop fronts. He began to be hungry again, and now he had only four annas. He stood outside a tea-shop, and looked at the people sitting at the small tables inside, drinking tea. He stood there looking for so long that the owner called out: "Why do you stand there looking, fool? Either come in and eat and drink or go away." He wanted to run away, but with a determined effort he entered. He stood quaking inside, until the owner laughed and said, "Do you have money?" He nodded. "Then go and sit down." And the owner pointed to a chair. Again panic took hold of him and he wanted to run, but he did not yield to it. He was very hungry. He sat on the edge of a chair and he asked one of the servers the price of a cup of tea. His voice sounded throttled as he spoke. The tea was an anna a cup. The server set it down before him with a clatter and he lifted it with shaking hands to his lips and drank it. As he swallowed the thick sweet liquid, strength began slowly to return to his limbs and the warmth of it filled his belly.

People began to come into the food-shop to sit at the

tables and eat and drink. The men who served called out in loud, cheerful voices, as they carried plates of food and drink. He mustered up his courage and asked for a plate of sev, and was astonished when it was brought to him. He was being served food and was eating it with all the others and nobody seemed to notice him at all—him or his untouchability. The skies were not opening, nor the earth cracking. The shopkeeper took the money he gave without so much as a glance at him. He was busy collecting money from all his customers and the coins clinked and jingled as he put them into the drawer.

All day Boda walked on the streets of the city. When night came he slept on the steps of the pedestal of a statue. In the morning he was woken up by the cooing of hundreds of pigeons that had settled on the statue. He began the day by relieving himself on the side of the street and washing and rinsing his mouth at a fountain. Then he began to walk again. But now he was hungry again and his belly had gone down and had stuck to his back. He walked down the street past the tall buildings and rows of shops until he came to the market place of the city, with its rows of shops where men sat cross-legged, selling all kinds of things—vegetables, fruits, groceries, clothes, trunks, cups and saucers, glasses, knives, locks, keys. Boda was open-mouthed with surprise to see the variety of wares spread out before him. At that early hour the shopkeepers were still only opening their shops and laying out their things. He stood and stared for a long while, until at last he heard a laughing voice calling him: "What are you staring for, you village lout?" and he started, a little ashamed. The shopkeeper beckoned to him and said: "If you are looking for work, I can give you work to do." He nodded. A doubt flickered in his mind and he wondered if the man would want to know his caste. But he did not mention caste at all and Boda remained silent. He hired himself to the grocer, for the wage of three rupees a month.

"I will work for you." he said. "But I am hungry and have no money. Give me a little now and I will pay back my debt." But this the man would not do.

So Boda had to work on a hungry stomach, carrying baskets of groceries for customers to their doorsteps. When he was carrying a sack of rice for a fat woman who lived on the third storey of a tall building, Boda felt dizzy and faint. As he lowered the sack upon the floor he tottered and fell into a faint. When he opened his eyes he felt cold water being splashed upon his face and saw someone looking down at him. He saw the fat woman's face—a coarse and ugly face with warts and ungainly growth of hair.

"Hey, hey there," she shouted, "are you ill? Get up, and tell me what is the matter."

"I am dying of hunger," Boda confessed. "For two days I have had no food."

"Poor fellow," said the woman and the others around her echoed her words. She brought out some stale bread and a can of lukewarm tea, which he devoured ravenously like an animal, scarcely looking up once.

When he had finished she gave him an anna, and he rose and turned to go. But she called him again and suddenly she threw him a silver four-anna piece. No one asked him his caste.

Boda worked for the grocer and his work allowed him little respite. But he came to know the alleys and by-ways and roads of the city and to understand the ways of city-people. Customers sometimes tipped him an anna or two or gave him leftover food but he was often starved and hungry. His clothes were in shreds. He slept on the bench outside the shop. At the end of the month the shopkeeper gave him two rupees and eight annas; he said he had kept back eight annas for the rent of the bench on which he slept. Boda felt he was being cheated, but he was not sure and answered nothing. He still earned small tips and with this money he was able to get some food and tea and even an occasional packet of beedies. He began to smoke beedies and he liked the taste and the feel of them. He began to be happy. Best of all was the feeling of being free of the tyrannies of life in his village among his people. He continued to work and earn, but he found that his needs were increasing. He began to go to the cinema. At first not very often, but after a while he found the cinema made him forget his sorrows and troubles, and he began to frequent the theatres. When he looked at the moving pictures his dreary life fell away from him. He felt he was a new man, and he sensed a great soaring happiness as he became the hero on the screen, riding in a motor car, or a horse, fighting and overcoming his enemies and winning the love of beautiful women. The cinema was like a new life he was living. It took all his earnings from him, and he had often to go hungry. But he did not mind very much. He took to wandering in the streets during the nights and came upon groups of men squatting under street lamps throwing dice or playing cards. He saw piles of coins exchanging hands. This seemed to him a good easy way to earn money to pay off his debt and to buy his needs, and so he began to play too. Sometimes he won, but often he lost, and there were fierce quarrels. During one of them he struck a man on the head so that he fell unconscious and bleeding at the mouth. Boda left them and fled in fear. He fled through the lamp-lit streets and just behind him he seemed to hear the sound of policemen's shoes. Somehow he escaped being caught this time and when morning came he was still free. But he was far from the market where he worked. He had forcibly taken from the man he had struck two rupees that he had won, and he still had the money in his pocket. It would last him if he was careful for a few days. He lay hiding near the staircase of a dark gloomy building. Here he slept for a day until he was discovered and chased away with threats and curses. He took to the streets again, and began to sleep under a great bridge. After a few days his fear began to leave him as his hunger began to return.

Then he wandered again in the streets until he came at last to the house of the woman for whom he had carried groceries the first day.

"Are you not the boy who robbed the grocer Kishenlal and fled?" the startled lady asked him.

Boda answered: "I was the grocer's servant but I did not rob him. He was a thief. He took work from me, and refused to pay me."

The woman said: "Why do you come here now?"

Boda said to her: "I will work in your household as your servant for a wage and for leftover food and shelter." The woman was in need of such a servant but she looked at Boda doubtfully.

"Will you engage me?" Boda asked impatiently and added: "I will work well for you. I will do any kind of work."

The woman did not answer and Boda began to think that she had no need of a servant. But at last she said, regarding him doubtfully:

"Before I engage you I must know your caste. We are high-caste people; our caste is nearly as high as the Brahman caste and I cannot let an unknown person work for me. My husband and I will not eat what has been touched and polluted by low-caste people."

This was the first time that he had been confronted with caste in the city, but he lied without hesitation and laughing inwardly, said: "I am a weaver by caste. In my village the weaver caste is almost as high as the Brahman, and we receive the sacred thread, as the Brahmans do. In the community feasts of the temple we sit in the outer hall to eat, and we mourn our dead for twelve days." When Boda spoke his tongue moved with ease, and his eyes did not flinch from the woman's face. "It is not easy to find good servants," he went on, looking at her steadily, "and it is even more difficult to find men of caste." The woman nodded. "If you are of the weaver caste then I will engage you."

Boda became her servant.

He stayed in the woman's house and entered her kitchen. He ground spices for her and cooked rice and even filled her waterpot.

She was pious and performed her prayer rituals three times a day after her bath. Boda brought her the foods she needed for worship and she, believing him to be of the weaver caste, accepted these things from his hands and ate the food he cooked and drank the water he had touched.

All the while Boda was speaking I had been listening quietly, with hardly a movement and hardly the quiver of an eyelid. But now when he told me this, I started violently crying out and protesting: "Oh my brother! Why did you deceive her? Why did you have to sin against this woman?"

Boda looked at me, mockery flickering in his eyes. "I wanted to see if indeed my touch could pollute. They ate the rice I cooked and believe me, they fattened on it. The water which I filled in the water-pot didn't change colour because I had filled it! The earth didn't shake; neither did the heavens fall!" And he threw back his head and laughed riotously.

"It was not right!" I cried out, scandalised. "Such deception is sin."

Boda blew out a puff of smoke and laughed. He held the beedi between his thumb and finger and stuck it back into his mouth between his teeth.

"Sin! Khah—sin," he retorted. "This is Kali Yuga, girl, the age of sin, the age of evil, of the mixing of caste!" He shrugged, still laughing. "For me this sin, as you call it, brought wages enough to keep my belly warm and silent. Besides each time I served these caste people their rice with my scavenger's hands it did my heart and spirit good."

That was my angry brother's revenge. I could not understand it then, I cannot understand it still. What did it gain him? For all his talk of its doing good to his heart and spirit, my brother continued a bitter, unhappy man. The taint of untouchability continued to be with him and there was a violence in his soul which tormented him.

He did not stay with the woman long. Every day he wandered over the streets and one day in his wanderings he met Govinda, who had been in the city for many years, having come as a little boy from his village one year when times were hard, and his father had been unable to pay his debts. The owner of the land which his father tilled threw Govinda's father out, and the old man returned to work on it as a labourer.

Govinda's father brought the boy one day to the landlord's house and offered him to the man as a servant. He would work for the landlord's son and daughter-in-law who lived in Bombay and his monthly salary would go towards repayment of the loan. So the boy worked for his master and mistress washing vessels, and clothes, sweeping the house, and mopping it, and cleaning shoes, and running errands. The woman of the house was shrill-voiced and hard-hearted, and abused the boy through the day and beat him often. He had very little to eat, and his wages went to repay his father's loan. Sick in body and heart, black and blue all over with the marks of the woman's heavy hand, Govinda ran away one night, and disappeared into the maze of alleys. She never found him until years later when he had grown. He learnt the ways of the city. He learnt to fend for himself, and to survive. He even acquired some education, for after a while he began to attend a school where boys and men gathered under a street lamp and learned to read and write. He learned enough to write a simple letter to his father and send him month by month a part of his earnings. Thus Govinda grew up a man of the city, of the world. He got a job in a cotton mill where giant spindles turned out yarn into cloth. He took the job because it carried many benefits, of which the most tempting was a room on the third storey of a vast building not far from the place of work. It was dark and damp, rat-infested; the plaster on the walls peeled continuously. In the rains the water soaked through the walls and roof where it did not leak; there were hundreds of people who lived in this building with him.

Now that he had a place of his own to live in, Govinda went home to the village, and got himself the bride his father had chosen for him. After he was married he prepared to return to the city with his new bride, his father and his sister. But the old man, now bent and feeble, had no wish at all to leave the village. He begged his son to leave him there, so that he could die where he had lived all his days. So Govinda left him in his village, and travelled back to the city with only his wife and his sister Ganga. Govinda's children were born in the city, in the room where they lived. There were six of them, each born within a year of the last, and now there were eight to feed on the earnings of one man. "We cannot live thus!" Govinda thought to himself, for the children were wretched, ill, hungry and dirty. There was no happiness in their life, and Govinda felt he had been foully cheated. Like hundreds of others he was heavily in debt, and his creditors swarmed the place and dogged his footsteps and left him no peace. His body grew weak and a cough racked him, because of the minute specks of cotton that he breathed in with air, and at night he was sleepless and miserable. One day he joined the group of workers in the mill who had banded themselves into a union. He went to the union meeting and listened to them. There were about twelve men together, and they brought him such a message of hope and courage and cheer that when he came away from that meeting Govinda felt transformed. He listened intently to their words. In passionate voices they told him about their union. The union leaders would go to their masters and present their grievances and demands to them. Alone, each was weak, but in a body there was strength, and even the powerful men who ruled them would have to bend and listen and concede their demands. "And if they don't concede?" someone asked. The men replied: "Ha! If they don't concede! If a thousand workmen said in one voice—'We will not work unless our voices are heard, unless our grievances are looked into and our wrongs righted—' What would our masters say to that, eh? They will concede soon enough?"

Govinda became a member of the union. He had a quick and energetic mind. He could read and write. He was honest and trustworthy. Soon he became an important member of the union. People listened when he spoke. It was at that time that Boda met him, and the two became friends. After a while Boda left the woman he served and secured with

Govinda's help a place in the Spinning Mill. He could not get a room to live in because all the rooms in the building were occupied, so Boda began to sleep in the space just outside Govinda's room. He cooked his rice on a little iron stove there, and at night he lay outside Govinda's door, and when morning came, the two went to work together. Govinda and Boda became friends; at the union meetings they sat together, and Boda was happy to live on Govinda's doorstep. The admiration and love that he felt for Govinda he had never felt for anyone before. When Govinda spoke Boda listened with rapt attention. When Govinda required work to be done, he was alert and sprang up to do it. There was no man, thought Boda, as wise, as generous, as great and as good, as Govinda. He was happy just to be with Govinda.

Boda admired Govinda tremendously. He imitated him unconciously and consciously, walked, talked and dressed like him. Govinda was like a god to him. And for the first time in his life Boda had a friend and knew happiness.

Govinda was one reason, of course, for Boda's happiness. But there was another also. That second reason was Ganga, Govinda's sister. Boda thought her the most beautiful creature in the world and began to dream of her day and night. He dreamed of the time when he would make her his wife. For now that he was free of his untouchability he decided that it would be no sin to ask Govinda for her hand. He moved in a sort of daze as he thought of how he would work and earn for her, of how he would know the intense happiness of being with her always. He dreamed of how he would rent a room where they would live, how in the evenings after his work they would go to the park and sit on the bench together. He dreamed of how he would take her to the cinema. He dreamed and dreamed.

He began to wait for her at the bottom of the staircase and to walk with her. He began to bring her small gifts—beads, ribbons, hair clips, bangles, and he pressed her to take them. In the beginning she would refuse, moistening her lips with the tip of her tongue, twisting and untwisting the end of her sari with nervous fingers. But she did not resist for very long, and when he begged her to accept his offering she would put out her hand and take his gift and run shyly from him. He was charmed by these ways of hers. He began to know every small detail of her face and to love it separately. She was the one, he told himself many times, who would cook for him and bear his children. He had a strange feeling that he had always known her, always through countless lives of the past. She had become all life to him, and as necesary to him as breath. She was the one, who, for him, would wipe out his past and create his future.

As Divali approached Boda began to make plans. The workers would be paid a bonus for the festival. The extra money would be very welcome indeed. There were six weeks still to go and Boda was living now in the future and for the future.

While he was thinking, the Union announced the great strike. It was Govinda who told them about it at one of the meetings. All the mill workers of Bombay were participating, said Govinda. It was to be a very big strike indeed. They were all to vote for the strike. They were the workers of the world. In their hands was the prosperity of the country. If they united they could change the world. Now they lived in misery, worse than rats in their holes. They were prisoners in shackles. If they united in action they would gain the whole world.

The strike was over the question of the Divali bonus. The

masters declared that business had been low. There had been no profits, they said, and so there would be no Divali bonus. Govinda spoke stirring words. "It is a lie." These men, he said, would make profit from the blood of their children and the sale of their wives. "No, friends do not believe them!" The workers clenched their fists and shook them and shouted out their approval. They voted for a strike. Boda sat staring helplessly. A strike meant a collapse of all his dreams. He felt no elation whatsoever at the decision. He was the only one whose hand did not shoot up at Govinda's word. Govinda observed this and later remarked on it.

Boda did not have a ready answer for him. He stammered and could not speak easily. He could not tell Govinda that a strike meant a long delay in the execution of his own plan. A strike meant hard days of tension, and anger. He could not work up tension inside him at all. His mind was full of gentle dreams. The thought of a strike made him unhappy and frightened him. He did not, did not, did not want a strike. He wanted to be with Ganga: he wanted to marry her and love her and find happiness. But he could not say all this to Govinda.

Govinda was disappointed in Boda. He had not expected to be let down by the man he had befriended. But he was too busy to bother. And the strike began. First there was a procession. More than twenty thousand mill workers walked in the procession demanding fair treatment, demanding a share in the profits they had helped to make. And my brother Boda walked in the procession, although he was not in favour of the strike. He walked because Ganga walked in the procession. She walked with Govinda's wife and the wives and sisters and mothers of the other workers. It seemed to Boda as he walked that here among the working folk of the city there was unity and brotherhood. No caste or religion divided them, and there were no people at all who were branded untouchable. Yet he wished that the strike had not been now. It upset his plans, and ruined his dreams.

"Those who are not with us are against us," Govinda shouted from a platform, and Boda trembled to think Govinda might be meaning him. He said it again darkly that evening when they sat in their room discussing the events of the day and their plans for the future.

"They are traitors to the workers' cause!" said Govinda. Boda saw Ganga's shadow in the passage outside the room, and he felt a tightness in his throat because of his love. Oh how he wished the strike had not been now! He could not bring himself to put his heart in it. Govinda spoke about the traitors contemptuously, the men who continued loyal to the bosses at a time like this. He called them ugly names.

"I spit on them," said Govinda and everyone shouted and clapped. Boda also clapped, but he wished as he saw Ganga's shadow, that the strike had not been now. And the clapping of his hands was very mechanical. There was much excitement at first among the strikers. Every day there were speeches, processions, oath-taking ceremonies and meetings. Every day the processions converged on the gates of the mill and the strikers squatted outside. There were police everywhere; many came to protect the workers who would not join the strike. Before the strike was three days old, some of the leaders were arrested and among them was Govinda. The police took them away and they were put into jail. Boda expected that Govinda's wife would be crushed under the shock. But he was wrong. Govinda's wife was an amazing woman. She feared no one, depended on no one. And Ganga stood by her. Together the two women continued to go with the other workers to the gates of the mill and squat there in silence, as they had been doing, refusing to work unless their demand for fair and human treatment was met. Boda marvelled to see the grit and spirit of these women. Life in the city was so different from life in Venugopalapuram—he might have been living in another world! And his heart beat high as he thought of Ganga, her courage, her intelligence, her beauty.

As the days passed things began to get difficult. At first Govinda's wife and Ganga had some savings between them to buy food for the children, but they came one day to the end of it. And the strike continued. A week went by without wages—eight, nine, ten days! The families began to show the effect of the strike. From two meals they came down to eating one meal. But that one meal grew thinner. The children began to whimper with hunger. Boda shared his savings with his friend's family. He had not wanted the strike, but he knew that it was important to hold out and not give in at this stage. Victory, they said, was in sight. The big masters were weakening, wavering. He wondered if that was so, and hoped it was. He had known hunger before, but it was agony to see Ganga reduced to skin and bones. And the children's cries wrung his heart.

On the eleventh day of the strike there was a riot. Stones were thrown. There was a clash outside the mill where Ganga and her sister-in-law were squatting with the other women. No one knew who started the riot, but Boda saw people running with sticks and iron rails in their hands. He saw bricks and stones flying; saw the police with their lathis; heard the shouting and the screaming. He realised that it was a riot between the strikers and the loyal workers who would not join them. And the sight of the bricks flying made him tremble to think what might happen to Ganga. If Ganga should be hurt!

Many people were hurt in the riot. Among them was not Ganga, but one of Govinda's children, a ten-year old girl who was coming to the mill site with the food she had cooked for her mother and aunt. No brickbat hit the little girl but as she was walking towards the gates where they were squatting with the other strikers, word went round that the police had started to shoot. Boda saw no guns, heard no sound of shooting, but he saw how the crowd in panic began to yell and rush and stampede. He found himself separated from Govinda's family, with whom up to then he had kept close, and pushed along with a frightened crowd. The bricks and stones were still flying and Boda was praying that Ganga would not be hurt. But he had lost Ganga in the stampeding crowd. And all around him the people were shouting and yelling.

He saw how people were thrown down and trampled on as the crowd made its frenzied way through the lane. And frightened cold to think what might happen to Ganga, he managed, as if by a miracle, to reach a wall. And it was there that he saw Govinda's little girl, Savitri. She had fallen down, and she was bleeding at the head.

He did not know then that it was Savitri. But the sight of the child let loose a volume of feeling in his heart and he knew he had to save her. He leaned against the wall with a demoniacal determination and he flung out his arms wildly, and shouted with all the power of his lungs. And two other men also from the rushing, stampeding crowd heard him, turned their heads, saw what was the matter, then put out their arms to support themselves against the wall. Then three others came and joined them while the crowd moved on like a herd of insane elephants. Others came and presently seven men had formed a protecting ring round the girl—against the frenzied rush of the crowd.

Boda would have picked up the girl but one of the men shouted: "Don't move. Don't move at all. Just stand still. Stand there and don't move." So he dug his feet in and stood with them, until presently the crowd's fury became less. And then Boda and his companions bent down and Boda lifted up the child, and discovered that it was Savitri.

"I know her," he said. "I will take her home."

He carried her in his arms and brought her home. He washed her wounds and was about to take her to the small dispensary outside the gates to the chawls when Ganga and the others came back. Ganga's sari was torn. Her hair had come loose. Her wrists were cut and bleeding where her glass bangles had broken, and Govinda's wife too was bruised and shaken. But when they saw Savitri they forgot themselves, and the mother began to weep.

"She is not badly hurt," Boda said, "She will be all right. I will take her to the dispensary." He lifted up the child. The women came with him. In answer to their questions Boda told them all that had happened. He thought he saw Ganga's eyes full of gratitude and pride and admiration. And he was glad he had been the one to save the little child and bring her home. Now he was sure that Govinda would give Ganga to him in marriage. "This is the city," he told himself. "In the city there are no caste distinctions. All are equal."

The day came when Govinda was released from jail. Govinda's wife had said many times that the strike would have to come to an end. The workers were suffering from hunger—true—but hunger was not a new thing. On the other hand the closure of the mills meant heavy losses for the owners—and this they would not allow to go on for too long. They would begin to think again. They did just as Govinda's wife had said. They called for negotiations, and the day came when they and the leaders among the workers sat at a table together to negotiate. One of the leaders was Govinda.

In Govinda's chawl there was rejoicing and jubilation at the news. Govinda had always been respected as one of the educated men. His word had always carried weight. Now he became a hero. He had led the strike. He had gone to jail. Now he would speak for his people, the workers. Govinda was garlanded. Rice was thrown over him. Arati lights were circled round his face. An old man brought fruit for him. They praised him and sang songs about him. They brought him their babies to touch and bless. They wished him success as he went with the others to the place of negotiations. He spoke to the bosses. For a week there were meetings and discussions. Govinda came home late each night and left early. Boda stayed with the family. Savitri grew better with each day. Finally agreements were signed. Govinda's signature was among the other signatures, and there was a great pride everywhere in his achievement.

And Boda made up his mind to ask him for his sister's hand, because during all these days he had come close to the family. Ganga had been good to him. Sometimes their eyes had met, his and hers, and he had seen—he was sure he had seen—tenderness in hers. He was sure she returned his love.

The thought of his untouchability did not seem important to him now after the great events in their lives together. "Here things are different," he told himself. "Here there no distinctions. We are workers and comrades in work." And he thought of how they had all marched side by side and stood together during the days of the strike.

So one day he spoke to Govinda. He took gifts for the family, some fruits and sweets and he approached his friend.

"I have something to tell you," Boda said. Govinda asked him to sit down. They drank tea together. They chewed betel leaf and nuts together. They smoked a couple of beedies together. They talked about the strike and the gains they had won. Govinda mentioned the incident about Savitri. In a voice that trembled slightly with emotion and gratitude, Govinda thanked Boda. "Why do you thank me?" Boda answered. "I did nothing that you would not do!" After a while Boda broached the topic of marriage, moistening his lips with his tongue because of his nervousness. He spoke fast and fearfully, and suddenly stopped overcome with fear and confusion. There was a dead silence, in which it seemed to Boda that he could hear his heart beat loud. The earth seemed to be spinning round him. Boda spoke of his desire to marry Ganga. He promised Govinda that he would be a good husband. He spoke and spoke, and then he stopped speaking suddenly, because there was no movement at all from Govinda. No movement, no answer. Boda stopped talking and stared at his friend. Govinda sat there, his jaw set, his eye turned away, saying nothing at all. It seemed such an eternity that Boda stared. At last Boda cried out: "Why do you not speak, my friend?" and his voice sounded thin as a reed pipe, very different from his voice as he knew it. "Why do you not speak?"

Govinda's face was like a mask. He said in a tight constricted voice: "Boda, we have been friends and comrades for many days now. We have worked and suffered together. And though I knew you for an untouchable, I never allowed that to come in the way of our friendship. You know it as well as I do."

Boda shrank to see the look on his face, shrank from hearing his words: "Let us remain friends, Boda," said Govinda. "I do not want to quarrel with you." Boda felt as if his stomach was dissolving leaving only a hole in the centre of his body. "Quarrel? Quarrel?" He whispered. "What should we quarrel about, Govinda?" But inside him the words— "though I knew you to be an untouchable"—kept hammering at every nerve of his being.

"Don't try my patience," Govinda answered. "Another man in my place would have whipped the life out of you."

Boda stared at him dumbly, holding the gifts in his trembling hands. "Though I knew you to be an untouchable—an untouchable...."

Suddenly Govinda shouted angrily, "You have the nerve—the audacity, scavenger and untouchable, did you think I did not know? What penalty is there for this insult?" Boda put his hand to his head and uttered a low cry. But Govinda paying no attention to him went on: "Did you think me a fool because we were kind? Or did you think we would not find out?" He glared savagely at Boda and continued: "No matter where he goes, a man's caste can never be hidden. It is part of him. You should know that." Boda began to weep. "In the city a man's caste does not matter," he sobbed.

"No," Govinda agreed, in a gentler tone. He averted his face when he saw Boda weep. "It does not. But you are a fool, Boda, if you do not understand that marriage is another thing altogether." Boda continued to weep silently and Govinda went on, "Marriage is a bond by which a man secures himself to his family and ancestors; to the roots out of which he was created. Marriage is different. Are you so stupid as not to know that?"

Desperately Boda asked: "Govinda, who made these rules, these chains?"

"I don't know," Govinda replied. "They have come down to us from the ancients. All I know is that we may not go against them."

Boda stared at the man who had been his friend and hero for so many months. Was this the same person? Suddenly he wiped his tears. "I will ask Ganga," Boda said with passion.

Govinda replied: "You lout, you bastard, you cleaner of filth, you dare to take her name! I would have you beaten to a pulp."

"I will ask Ganga, I will ask Ganga—" Boda repeated as he went away. And he waited at the bottom of the staircase at the time he knew Ganga would come down. She did not come that day, nor the next, and he cursed and swore and wept. On the fourth day the child Savitri was coming down the steps with a bag in her hand. He accosted her smiling. But she turned her face away. "Where is your aunt? Why does she not come?" whispered Boda.

Savitri sniffed, turning up her little nose and said haughtily: "My mother told me you are untouchable and a cleaner of filth, that I was not to talk to you or allow you to touch me."

"Where is Ganga?" Boda asked, impatiently, "Tell me that."

"Gone," said the girl. "She has been sent to the village to her husband's house. She will not come back—never. And you are not to talk to me—you are untouchable." She lifted up her head high in the air and sailed off, taking care not to let her clothes brush him as she went.

Boda felt that his existence had been wiped away completely and he was just nothingness and nothingness. He made his way back to the village. He was thin as a skeleton. His eyes were bloodshot. There was a fever in his body and a sickness in his soul. He cursed himself. He cursed Ganga and Govinda. He cursed the caste people, and he cursed the untouchable people. He cursed his fate.

That was Boda's story as he told it to me. He told it in fragments and I pieced it together. I do not think he ever forgot the girl Ganga or forgave Govinda. He had been a bitter, angry youth when he left us. But now there was no sanity, it seemed, left in him. His eyes were filmed over with a never-dying hatred and anger.

I fed him as well as I could. I brought him medicines for his fever and cough from Father Pierre. He ate the food, but he cursed and swore and refused the medicine, because, for some reason I could not fathom, he hated Father Pierre. He abused him and reviled him until I could bear it no longer and ran out of earshot. Only Soma could calm his anger, for there was a bond between them that had existed even before he had left us and gone. In the end Soma took him to stay with her, and he went. She was good to him. She sat by him and spoke to him. She was stern and kind to him by turns. Sometimes she said things to him that even made him smile—a bitter, twisted dry sort of smile that made my heart go cold inside me. He smiled when she spoke of the junior priest and mimicked his talk, laughing heartily herself as she broke off pieces of sugarcane with her teeth.

He was sick with the tuberculosis sickness that he had caught in the city. We saw how day by day the disease ravaged his body and ate up his strength. But to the end he continued thus, his anger burned in his eyes and heart. To the end he neither forgot what he had suffered nor forgave those who had caused his sufferings.

He would not stay at home. Even with his fever and his cough he would go out, never saying where he went or for what purpose.

But the world outside was changing. One day the Acharya announced in the school that he had something important to tell us. He assembled the students together and said: "Listen carefully to what I am going to read out."

"Listen," he said, and as we waited, hushed and expectant, he read out to us the news of the fast that Mahatma Gandhi was going to undertake to atone for the sin of those who put up barriers between people and called their brothers untouchable. We listened open-mouthed and open-eyed, and the Acharya went on to explain how Mahatma Gandhi had called out to the people to open the doors of the temples and allow the Harijan folk to enter with everyone else to worship. The Acharya folded his newspaper. "It is a great event," he said, "nothing like this has happened in hundreds of years. It is the dawning of a new, golden age—the beginning of Rama Rajya. Injustice will be no more and all men will henceforth be brothers."

"Mahatma Gandhi Ki Jai. Mahatma Gandhi Ki Jai!" I shouted after him and the others who came to him for their lessons also cried out "Mahatma Gandhi Ki Jai" in great joy. I asked the Acharya if I could take the newspaper to the untouchable quarters to read the news out to the people, and he agreed.

They gathered around me to listen. And I spoke to them in the Acharya's words with conviction: "It is the dawn of a new golden age," I said. "Injustice will be no more, and all men will be brothers." I waited to hear the shouts of approval and joy—but none came: the listening people moved uneasily. I glanced at Kantanna's face. There was a troubled, unhappy frown on his brow.

"The Mahatma is a man of God," he said. "Then why does he do these things? Why does he upset the laws the ancients have made? The laws are the foundations of our society—and yet, and yet no one can deny that the Mahatma is a man of God."

Ponchu looked at me grimly and said: "You are mad—you are blind. Why won't you listen, Lachi, why won't you listen? These sins which are being committed will bring destruction on the world." There were several people who echoed what Granny Ponchu said. "The temple may not be defiled," they said, "or the sin will be on our heads."

Ponchu had no doubts. As I was still listening to her, Boda snatched the paper from me and read it aloud in a loud voice and derisive tone. He spat angrily in the direction of the temple, and said:

"And what will you get by entering this temple? Will it get you food? Will it fill your hungry belly?"

"Perhaps, perhaps it is a step in the right—direction?" Kantanna put in slowly, hesitantly. "Perhaps when they worship together men will see that we are all one—"

"One, *one!*" cried Boda. "How can we be one? How can there ever be oneness between us? We are not one at all, and we shall never be one with these pot-bellied thieves who have insulted us, spat on us, destroyed us. Do you think that the walls of hate that have stood between us for so long can be broken by a fool's fasting?"

Soma stood beside him. Her eyes were defiant. He continued, "These people need to be kicked, to be beaten, to have their faces blackened. What have we to do with their temple? The temple!" He spat again viciously. "Enter into—set fire to the temple. Burn it down!" He stopped as he began to cough. He coughed and coughed. Soma put her arm round him. "He is a fool. He is mad," shouted several voices, and many people shook their fists at him, but most stood dazed unable to understand him, and unable too to understand the Mahatma's strange resolve. "This is no ordinary happening," they said, as they dispersed. "Out of a single cause who knows what and how many results will flow out?"

Boda began to cough blood. Soma took him home and forced him to lie down. But he would not be quiet.

The next day the Gandhi men had a meeting at the Banyan Tree Square. I had to go. I could not stay away. A force I could not resist dragged me to the meeting. The Acharya led the meeting and spoke to the people who had collected. He spoke to them in stirring words. His voice rang with the intensity of his passion. "A new world is being born my friends," the Acharya said, and he spoke of the brotherhood of all people under the sun. After a while Radha took up and continued: "Come, join us in this great task of bringing the Mahatma's message to life," she called, raising her hands as if she was a goddess come to life. "The Brotherhood of man is about to be restored. Come, walk with us. Let us stand outside the temple until the miracle takes place and the doors open." Her eyes shone and there was a smile on her lips. She seemed to be in a dream. "Mahatma Gandhi Ki Jai!" shouted a third worker and many voices cried out after him, their voices alive and ringing. But many held back, some had doubt in their faces; in others there was indifference. And there were some who looked at the Teacher with anger, and shook their fists, their sticks, their umbrellas at him.

Something happened to me when I saw the Teacher's flaming eyes and heard his words. My entire being seemed to throb with life. I came under a spell, as if possessed by the Goddess. It seemed to me that I must put down whatever I was doing and follow him and the Mahatma, and do what they asked. Suddenly it seemed to me that if we could enter the temple and see the idol and worship it alongside the caste folk, then, as the Acharya had promised, all the wrongs of the world would be righted, all the injustices remedied.

Father Pierre spoke too. "Do you not see that God does not belong to the priests and caste folk alone? Do you not see that he must not be imprisoned, that all must see his face, that all must hear the music of his flute!" How earnest and gentle his voice was, how kind his face. But as he finished the sentence there came flying in the air a ball of wet mud which hit his face and splashed on his cassock. I screamed. I saw that it was Boda, my brother who had flung the mud at him. He had come too.

"You aren't one of us," Boda panted. "What have you to do with us? False Priest, foreigner!"

So far the untouchable people had been silent, but at this point there came an angry murmur from some of them. It seemed to me that Kantanna and others would have sprung on Boda and torn him to pieces had Father Pierre and the Gandhi men not held them back. Boda continued angrily addressing the Acharya as Soma pulled him away: "And you scholar with your smooth words and false tongue, do you think we don't know you and your tricks? A curse on you and—."

Boda was led away, but there were still two or three angry scavengers who stood there, cursing and declaring that between the caste folk and us there would never be anything but the walls of hatred that the centuries had erected.

I realised that during the days that Boda had spent with us he had not been idle. Even with the illness racking his body and death staring him in the face he had not been idle. He had been speaking to people, stirring up angry thoughts in their hearts. The hatreds he had roused showed in their eyes and faces and in their clenched fists. On the other side of us some way away stood the caste folk of Venugopalapuram, the weavers, the carpenters, the tradesmen. There were also the priests with their faces and bodies painted with the priestly signs. They were all the upholders and interpreters of ancient law and tradition, the guardians of the temple and the keepers of the gods. They too did not approve of what the Mahatma was doing and were seething with anger and bitter abusive words. They too were warning us of the bitter consequences of letting loose these forces of change.

I stood between the groups, no more shy or hesitant, but throbbing with my enthusiasm, sure that the Gandhi men and I would put right all the wrongs in the world.

Radha held in her hands the saffron, white and green flag. Presently she sang a song about the new dawn, and the coming of a new age. And the Teacher and all of us took up the chorus and sang after her. The Acharya said: "Today miraculous things will happen. Come join us, friends. We shall enter the temple today with the Harijans and all the heavens will rejoice." He looked round: "Who—who will walk with us?" he cried in his passionate voice." There will be a procession today to the Venugopalapuram temple, which we shall cause to be opened. Who will walk with us?"

I stepped up. My face was burning with excitement. My limbs were trembling. Sai moved close to me, whispering: "I will come too." Then Kantanna said in his hesitant way "Who can understand the heart of a Mahatma? If the Mahatma wants it to be so then who am I to contradict him?" and he too came up and joined us.

"You are mad," cried Ponchu again desperately. "You will bring about destruction! Oh you will bring about ruin!" And from the other side where the caste folk stood came loud and angry voices: "What is this madness? Do you want to destroy the world by this sin?" But their voices were drowned in the shouts of the Gandhi men: "Mahatma Gandhi Ki Jai!"

More and more people joined us. There was a procession. It grew in size. More and more people joined it. No one knew from where they came, but the procession went on, and we marched at the head of it—Acharya, Radha and I.

"Did you not work for the eradication of untouchability?" they asked me, where I sat mourning Kittu's death and they fumbled with their notebooks and pencils as they waited to hear my answer. "Did you not work for Temple Entry?"

Yes, I walked with the Gandhi men at the head of the procession on the day when the doors of the Venugopalapuram temple were opened to us, the untouchable folk, whom Mahatma Gandhi called Harijans, Children of God—the same temple where they murdered my child, my Kittu, because he had entered to worship. The Acharya said: "It is a great day—seven hundred years ago was this temple built and today its doors are to fall open to the children of God.

Today we see arising the glorious sun of a new dawn!"

I lifted my eyes and I saw its gopuram shining in the sunshine, with all the gods and goddesses upon it, dancing, meditating, praying, making love, riding horses and tigers, taming elephants, making war. And then we entered through it. The Acharya took one arm of mine and Radha took another. You cannot falter now, something kept saying inside me. I found myself walking with them across the temple yard with its mighty peepul tree. And so we went up the steps of the temple. At the last step I stopped. I stood rooted to the spot unable to move. And time, the past, the present and the future whirled about me. I seemed to hear voices of all the gods and all the devils, all the people that were and had been and would be in the future, crying out: "What are you doing? Have a care. To go against what the ancients have laid down is a sin. To break the law is a sin. To deny tradition is a sin. And the consequences of sin...."

"Bharat Mata Ki Jai! Mahatma Gandhi Ki Jai! Long live Change," cried the Acharya and hundreds of voices cried out the words after him.

"Long live Change," Radha shouted.

"Was it a sin? Sin!" cried my fragmented, tortured mind, "We are committing sin. Are we not the unclean ones? What right have we to enter the temple that for hundreds and hundreds of years has been the bastion of the law of the ancients?" I began to sweat and tremble. I grew cold. "Let me go back!" I cried. "I must not, I cannot enter, I am untouchable, a scavenger." I can hear my voice crying out the words as I sit here now. They burst from me in a wild shriek. "Let me go. If I sin, I will eat the fruit of that sin. Let me go. Let me go." And I turned. But the Acharya held me on one side and Radha held me on the other. They would not let me go. "We shall be destroyed," I cried.

"Move on," said the Acharya. "We are at the end now." The crowd pressed from behind and suddenly I was lifted over the great stone threshold. There before us were the lights twinkling in the place of worship, around the image of Venugopala, the Flute Player. Suddenly bells began to ring. Suddenly voices began to sing the name of God. And suddenly before I knew it we were before the idol and my eyes saw the high priest there with the great arati in his hands. He turned and faced us once. Not a muscle of his stern face moved, but his eyes seemed to say: "What has to happen will happen. This is the age of sin, and who are we to try to prevent what the fates have ordained?" And he turned back to the idol and loudly chanting the prayers and ringing the bell, he performed the arati, so that in the glow of the lamps we who stood there saw with our own astonished, incredulous eyes the Flute Player and the smile on his lips. It was a miracle that the Flute Player worked that day. Surely it was a miracle. For the sight of him in all his beauty and all his glory was our salvation. Suddenly it seemed to me that my eyes opened that for so long had been blind: suddenly all barriers, all walls, all the great structure that the ancients had built was no more. I seemed to be floating in a sea of surging joy: all the wrongs of the world seemed to have been wiped away, and I heard around me and inside me the music of the flute. So I stood that day, alongside the Acharya and Radha, my young heart bursting.

"The world will never be the same again," said the Acharya to each of us, as the priests distributed the prayer offerings. His eyes were shining with pride and triumph. "All men will hereafter know themselves to be brothers. Mahatma Gandhi has worked a great deed. History will record the glory of this day that all men have stood before God as brothers. Mahatma Gandhi Ki Jai."

"Jai," shouted the people. "Jai, Jai, Mahatma Gandhi Ki Jai!"

A story that Kantanna used to tell came back to me as I gazed at the idol in the temple, and ate the sweetened rice.

One day, (so the story went) long, long ago, in this very temple a terrible thing happened. The idol disappeared. The night before, when the gates were barred and the doors locked, it had been there, but in the morning when the priests came for the ritual it had gone from the pedestal on which it stood, and only the pedestal remained. And stranger than anything was this, that the gold and silver and jewel-encrusted ornaments lay on the ground—unheeded—only the Flute Player's image was gone. It was a terrible thing to happen; The priests and the elders were in a panic. For it was believed that the prosperity of the land around rested on the image of Venugopala. There was a great search for the idol through the length and breadth of the land, but there was no sign of it anywhere. Worship came to a stop. When worship ceased, evil began to creep over the land; famine and flood, plague and pestilence, banditry and thieving. Life was no more safe. The cows ceased to yield and children died at the dry breasts of their mothers.

Then the people came to the chief priest, Krishnamachari, demanding to know what steps he was taking to recover the idol. They threatened to tear him to pieces if it was not restored. They would give him three nights, they said, and three days, and if he failed to recover the idol then let him beware. Krishnamachari sent messengers out once more, travelling on foot and horseback to every likely place, but on the evening of the second day the image had still not been found. He grew desperate and in his desperation he remembered God and prayed to him for help. Now that night he had a dream. He heard the laughing voice of a child calling, "Have you searched in the untouchables' section, my chief priest?" He recoiled at that, for he was a man of the highest caste and the purest blood and had never been defiled even by the shadow of an untouchable in all his life. And that is what he told God:

"Lord, how can I go among the untouchables, I who am a twice-born priest of high caste, Lord, don't ask me to do this. Do not torment me!" But the laughing voice only repeated, "Go, look in the scavengers' quarters."

What was he to do then? Morning came, and resigning himself to his bitter fate he turned his unwilling feet in the direction of the scavengers' quarters. The scavengers' quarters were far from the village. He was tired with walking in the heat, and by and by he felt an agony of thirst. He simply could not understand why he was being punished in this dreadful way.

When he reached the first hut in the untouchables' quarter, it was noon. He stood outside and called: "Is anyone there?" An untouchable woman came out, and seeing him, and the sacred thread on his body and the caste marks on his brow, uttered a cry of surprise. "Where is your man?" he demanded. She clasped her hands humbly and told him he was working, scavenging in the next village and would soon be back. He wondered how long he must wait here in this unclean place, and again he wondered what sin he had committed that he was being punished in this manner. After a while his thirst was so great that he could not bear it—and yet he dared not return to the village or the temple where the furious mob waited for him. In desperation at last, he crept nearer and asked the woman for water to drink, whispering: "I am dying of thirst. Give me water, but keep it a secret: no one must know that I have fouled myself drinking from your hands!"

The woman nodded humbly and brought him water and he drank while she poured. And though it was water fouled by her touch, he was surprised to find that it not only refreshed every nerve of his being, but that it tasted sweet in his mouth.

"The sun is hot, Swami," said the woman kindly. "Come and sit down under this poor and humble thatched roof. It is cool here." He glared at her angrily, thinking she was laughing at him. But she was not laughing.

He went in growling: "You mustn't speak about this to anyone. If people come to know that the priest has entered an untouchable's home and drunk water from unclean hands then I cannot imagine what would happen." The untouchable scavenger's wife nodded solemnly in agreement. She left him and went in, backing slowly away, to attend to her tasks and he stayed there waiting, remembering his dream, for it came back to him vivid and more real than so-called reality. It seemed to him that he had to wait endlessly and the children of the quarters came and stood around him. He shooed them away, but they came back again and again like troublesome flies. In the end, because he was tired and because he felt a strange loneliness he allowed them to stand and stare at him. After a while he permitted himself to smile at a child. He was surprised to find that she was so like his own granddaughter had been, a child who had died a few years ago. The children laughed and chattered around him and presently the little girl who was like his dead grandchild moved up to him and began to talk in her baby lisp: "Grandfather, O Grandfather," she addressed him. The scavenger woman of the house heard her and stepped out.

"Go away!" she waved her hand at them. "You must not

be familiar: go, go before you feel the weight of my hand."

"No, let her be," said the priest, surprised at himself. "Let her be! She is doing me no harm."

But the woman had already slapped the little girl and boxed her ears. The child cried out in pain, and the priest forgot himself (as he did in his own home when his daughters or daughters-in-law slapped their young ones). He put out his hand and rescued the child from her anger and soothed her as he would have done his grandchild. It happened before he could stop himself and tell himself she was untouchable. The child clung to him and soiled his sacred thread; her up-turned, tear-stained face was exactly like the face of his grandchild who was dead. And he found himself thinking strange thoughts. "Yes," he was thinking, "my sacred thread has been fouled but still the heavens have not struck me dead; the sun has not fallen from the sky, the planets haven't tumbled down and the earth hasn't collapsed! All continues to be as it had been!"

But he was growing impatient. "Will your man never come?" he asked the woman angrily, "I have important matters to discuss with him."

"He will come, master," the woman assured him, knocking her head on the ground before him. "He will come, I beg pardon; I will fall at your feet." Then the priest asked her if she knew anything about the idol and explained to her why he had come.

She shook her head, frightened at the thought of such a heinous crime as the theft of the Lord's image from the temple. "There is no idol here, master," she answered him, "We have no stone image. I fall at your feet, master, the dust of your feet I put on my head." What was to be done? I will face the anger of the people, the priest thought miserably. After all, one day we must all die. What worse than that can

Children of God

happen? I have failed, it seems, but not for want of effort.

He decided to leave and began to walk down the path. He had not walked many steps, when the children who danced alongside him pointed in the distance and shouted: "There he comes, and with him our Venu."

The untouchable scavenger man whom Krishnamachari had gone to meet was approaching and just behind him walked another who seemed like his servant carrying his broom and pan. Now Krishnamachari began to make haste to reach the scavenger, who seeing him, fell on the ground and kissed the dust. But Krishnamachari did not notice him. His eyes were on the boy, the dark youth who was walking beside him, carrying his broom and pan: it was no other than the Flute Player, the Deity of his temple, Venugopala, and he walked with the scavenger and carried his broom and pan. There was no mistaking him—for Krishnamachari had performed so many rituals every day for so many years before that image of the Flute Player that its face was imprinted on his heart and mind. And when he saw the Deity whom he had served all these fifty years thus degraded, his anger welled up in him and he cried out in a choking voice: "Lord, why have you come here among these unclean creatures to be degraded and fouled and shamed? What are you doing here, O you who rule the three worlds, whose beauty and power, whose compassion and glory are infinite and everlasting?"

The Flute Player smiled and said softly: "Krishnamachari, high priest of the temple, did you not know that I have always lived here among these people? Did you not know that my home has always been here?"

Krishnamachari shook his head, puzzled: "But the temple—" he stammered, "have you been deceiving us then, Lord?" he cried pathetically, "Have you been playing another of your jokes on us?"

The Flute Player gesturing with his lotus hands said: "Don't blame me, Krishnamachari; you have been deceiving yourself, praying and making offerings to an idol of stone. What could I do? How could I help it if you shut your eyes and made yourselves blind? Can you not understand that I was not to be held prisoner in stone? Can you not see that no one can hold me except with their love and devotion? These people cried out to me in their need and they loved me and I had to answer their call."

"But—but—but," the priest blurted out, his face red with rage, "My Lord! My Lord—these people are untouchables, how can you live among them? They—they make you work, they let you soil your gracious hands with their filthy scavenging—I will not have it! I cannot bear it!"

"For all your learning, Krishnamachari," said the Flute Player, "you are ignorant as a child." There was gentle pity in his voice. "For all your learning and your knowledge of the Vedas your mind is like a little empty shell, holding nothing of value."

Krishnamachari drew himself up haughtily. He did not like to be told even by the Deity that he was ignorant. "I am a Shastri," he reminded the Flute Player coldly. "I have spent my entire life learning the Vedas and the Scriptures." At that the Flute Player laughed a musical, merry laugh.

"What is the use of a lifetime—even of many lifetimes of knowledge—if your heart has not learnt love and compassion?" To which the priest had no ready answer, but he was very sore at the way things were going. At last he said, with something like irritation in his voice:

"Whatever that may be, I have found you now and you must return with me, for the temple is empty without you and how can the people serve you if you are not there?"

"But I am there and yet not there," the Flute Player said twinkling.

"That is no answer," snapped the priest. His patience was reaching its breaking point with this youth who refused to see that the matter was of importance. "What answer shall I give the waiting people?"

"But my place has always been here," the Flute Player assured him earnestly: "Did you not know that while you worshipped my stone image, I have always lived here with my devotees?" He seemed in no mood to lay down the broom and pan and to come home to the temple with the priest. Krishnamachari felt utterly thwarted and did not know what to do: just as he was becoming desperate the Flute Player took pity on him and said at last like a wilful child laying down a condition: "I will come into the temple if they too may come with me." He pointed to the scavengers who stood around them. Krishnamachari gaped at him wide-mouthed and incredulous.

"My Lord, My Lord!" cried the unhappy old man on the point of tears, "What is this you ask?" But the Flute Player only smiled his disarming, extraordinarily beautiful smile and would not say a word more. "Is the temple to have no idol then?" cried Krishnamachari. At that the face of the Flute Player lighted up as if a sudden thought had come to him, a sudden way out of this difficult situation. "If it is my *idol* you wanted, why did you not say so?" he laughed. That would not have been difficult.

Krishnamachari's heart stirred with hope. He listened keenly: "Go," said the Flute Player. "You will find my idol where it has always been—as if it had never vanished from there. Go and recite your learned mantras before it, flourish the arati lights around its stone face. Bathe the stone image in milk and water and smear sandal paste and vermilion upon its cold form. Adorn it with jewels and prostrate yourself before it. As for me, I shall be with my devotees, and we shall enter the temple together or not at all."

Now Krishnamachari was so worried about the ritual worship, that he only half-heard what the Flute Player said. And what he did hear was the promise that the idol would be where it had always been. When he heard that, he was relieved, for now he felt his purpose had been accomplished. He fled from the untouchable quarters, not waiting to thank the Flute Player or anyone. He ran to tell the waiting people that a miracle had been worked and the idol had been restored in all its dazzling beauty. In his joy he forgot all things including the Flute Player whom he left behind, and who called out to him: "Go to your temple, Krishnamachari. As for me I will not enter until my brothers here also enter with me!"

When Krishnamachari reached Venugopalapuram he purified himself of his pollution and entered the temple. There stood the idol in its perfection. The people blessed Krishnamachari and praised him and said it was a miracle he had brought about. They crowded into the temple for the morning rituals, which he performed punctiliously for he was very learned, and very systematic and had been trained for his duties for many, many years. And so now, once more the temple bells rang and the mantras were recited and all was as it had been before.

I sit now alone with my memories, and Kittu my son, the light of my life, more precious to me than my eyes, Kittu has gone.

Grief has turned now to memories, and all my days my memories will haunt me. The idol stands in the temple of

Venugopalapuram, as the Flute Player had promised that day long ago in the untouchable quarters. The priests, painted and bare-bodied, circumambulate chanting prayers to it and making their mystic gestures. "I worship Madhava. I worship Keshava. I worship Sri Krishna. You are my refuge, you are my salvation. You are the Creator, the Preserver, the Destroyer. You are the Saviour of sinners. You are the help of the helpless, the wealth of the poor, the strength of the weak, the fount of all virtue, of mercy, of justice, of kindness, of love. You reject none." They chant on and on and on and the bells ring and they bathe the idol in milk and water and dress it in silks; they adorn it with flowers and jewellery, burn incense, offer it food, offer it money, gold and silver, pearls, diamonds. And in the night they sing it to sleep, again chanting their learned Sanskrit mantras.

While outside my Kittu is stripped and tied to the tree, beaten and burned to death, because he is a scavenger and an untouchable. And laws are made and there is talk of the brotherhood of man.

But what are laws but words. And what good are words. Will they change men's hearts?

Will they bring my Kittu back to me?